1986

THE PRAGMATIC PHILOSOPHY
OF WILLIAM JAMES

The Pragmatic Philosophy of William James

Ellen Kappy Suckiel

UNIVERSITY OF NOTRE DAME PRESS
NOTRE DAME   LONDON

Library of Congress Cataloging in Publication Data

Suckiel, Ellen Kappy.
The pragmatic philosophy of William James.

Includes bibliographical references and index.
1. James, William, 1842-1910.   I. Title.
B945.J24S83   191   81-21993
ISBN 0-268-01548-1   AACR2

Manufactured in the United States of America

FOR
JOSEPH W. SUCKIEL

Contents

Preface

WILLIAM JAMES STANDS AS one of America's leading philosophers. He is one of the most articulate and effective spokesmen for what has been historically this country's most important and influential philosophical movement—pragmatism. While James has been highly regarded as a philosopher, and while deference is consistently paid to his importance in America's philosophical heritage, he has received far less attention in the way of technical philosophical commentary than would normally be expected. James is most often considered in the context of philosophical or intellectual history. Commentators tend to provide an exegesis of his more important pragmatic doctrines, but do not engage in a detailed examination and assessment of his reasons and arguments. The relative paucity of close work on James is due in part to the fact that he has often been regarded as an insightful but erratic philosopher, whose pragmatism does not represent a closely argued or integrated philosophical system.

It is true that in many of his writings James abandoned most of the accouterments that are characteristic of technical philosophers. For the most part, he did not involve himself in the full, painstaking articulation of his own considered positions, or in clarifying or making explicit the ways in which various aspects of his philosophy relate and support one another as parts of a systematic whole. His most influential writings appear in the form of semipopular lectures where his vivid pictorial imagination and dramatic mode of expression

tend to cloak the carefully wrought deliberations behind his claims. Moreover, it is well known that James
was inclined to take his philosophy piecemeal. In any
given article or lecture, the points he chose to develop
and defend, and the weight he placed on any particular aspect of his philosophy, frequently were affected
by his assessment of the concerns of his immediate
audience, the sorts of objections he anticipated, and the
particular polemical purpose he had in view. Indeed,
James was inclined even to reject logic when he felt it
interfered with philosophical insight. The result is a
thinker who is frequently contradictory, and in whom a
clear and coherent philosophy is difficult to trace. It is
no wonder, then, that there is considerable disagreement among scholars about the meaning and value of
his pragmatism.

But, in fact, as a philosopher James was far more
careful and systematic than he led his readers to believe. I have written this book as a comprehensive critical study of James's pragmatism. I have tried to show
that once we identify his most considered intentions, a
careful and thorough examination of James's pragmatic writings yields a coherent vision. This vision, whatever its difficulties, is the result of a consistent philosophical methodology, the elements of which relate in
sophisticated and conceptually integrated ways. My
purpose is to analyze and assess James's arguments and
proposals, and ultimately to establish the value of his
pragmatism as a technical and systematic philosophy.

This book would never have been written without
the help of Joseph W. Suckiel, who read the manuscript, and with whom I have had many extensive and
productive discussions about James. I have profited
immeasurably from his philosophical perspicacity and
uncompromising logical and stylistic rigor, as well as
his natural sympathy for James's point of view. His un-
faltering commitment to the project has been a source
of great support. I would like to express my thanks to
H. S. Thayer for his help at various times while this
work was being written, including his incisive com-

ments on various portions of the manuscript. Thanks are also due to M. G. Singer, who helped to make me aware of the richness of James's philosophy, and who provided valuable comments on several chapters. Whatever mistakes remain in this work, are, of course, my own. I am grateful to my parents, Jack and Lilyan Kappy, who have fostered this book in many important ways. I have gained much from the superb students in my William James seminar at the University of California, Santa Cruz, who through their dedication and interest have consistently confirmed my belief in James's importance. Shelley Starr, Betsy Wootten, and other past and present members of the Kresge College, UCSC, steno pool, impeccably typed various versions of the manuscript. This research was generously supported by fellowships and Faculty Research funds granted by the University of California, Santa Cruz.

Chapter 5 appeared in *Transactions of the Charles S. Peirce Society*, 15, no. 4 (Fall 1979). Portions of Chapter 3 appeared in the *Southern Journal of Philosophy*, 16, no. 1 (Spring 1978). I would like to thank the editors of these journals for permission to use this material.

Throughout this book, instead of using the expressions "he or she," "his or her," etc., I have used as generic terms "he," "his," etc. I found that in the present context any other stylistic alternative was ultimately too distracting to the reader.

Santa Cruz, California
April, 1981

1. James's Pragmatism as a Systematic World-View

WILLIAM JAMES FELT THAT one of the crucial features of a worthwhile philosophy is that it make a real connection with life. He considered philosophy, when properly executed, to be preeminently an expression of human interests and ideals, and a reflection of the concrete empirical conditions of our existence. But to hold such a view necessitates that one's philosophy be built around a particular conception of human nature. James conceives of persons as dynamic and vital centers of purposes and goals. His view of human nature is understood best when seen in contrast to the highly rationalized conception of the person which has held a prestigious place in the minds of many philosophers throughout history. Plato, for example, in the *Phaedrus*, portrays the soul of a human being as having three parts. The metaphor he uses to convey his idea is that of a charioteer being drawn by two horses. The two horses represent the spirited and appetitive elements of the soul, and the charioteer represents the rational element.[1] The metaphor is used to show the emotional and conative aspects of a person to be properly under full control of rational judgment. For Plato a person's proper end is to use his reason to control the spirit and appetite and to direct and guide them to appropriate ends—ends which reason sets.

There have always been some philosophers who have reacted against such a view. In the eighteenth century,

1

David Hume, for instance, argued against this conception of the dominant status of reason, but he did so more on the basis of the principles of his epistemology than by appeal to scientific knowledge of human nature.[2] But now the well-worn Platonic view of man has been undermined by modern science. Biological and psychological findings have made a progressively stronger case for the considerable extent to which human thought and behavior are governed by non-rational causes. Many have come to accept that desires, hopes, needs, fears, commitments, and the like make their own irreducible contribution to the rich texture of human life, and that the intellectual functions of human beings should not be considered properly predominant under all conditions.

Under the impact of nineteenth-century Darwinism, James was powerfully influenced by a biological model of human nature. He pictures the human being as a striving, goal-positing, interest-fulfilling organism, whose most important characteristic is his volitional appropriation and projection of ends. Indeed, far from being like the charioteer holding the passions in line and determining their appropriate limits, James sees the rational and cognitive faculties of human beings to be subservient to the spirited and emotional aspects of our nature. This means that the venerable intellectual functions are not self-sufficing or self-justifying, but are worthwhile only in the context of specific practical ends. Human consciousness, for James, is thoroughly teleological. Human cognitive activities—concept formation, belief acquisition, theory construction, and the like—function like tools which are limited and molded by the individual's preferences, desires, goals, and interests. The individual's goals themselves have the status of posits on James's view—they themselves neither require nor receive justification. Cognitive behavior is both motivated and, ultimately, justified by the individual's own internal and personally appropriated programs. We cannot think about anything without taking some sort of stand about what is desirable:

> The mind [is] an essentially teleological mechanism. I
> mean by this that the conceiving or theorizing faculty . . .
> functions *exclusively for the sake of ends* that . . . are set by
> our emotional and practical subjectivity altogether. It is a
> transformer of the world of our impressions into a totally
> different world—the world of our conception; and the
> transformation is effected in the interests of our volitional
> nature, and for no other purpose whatsoever.[3]

This teleological conception of mind is one of the
single most important principles in James's philosophical system, having wide-ranging implications throughout his thought. Indeed, as we shall see throughout this
book, virtually all other aspects of James's philosophy
utilize this conception of mind as a guiding principle.
James considers philosophy itself most importantly a
teleological product, a result of individual creative
energies and temperaments, which is to be judged by
reference to its adequacy in serving human ends. As
such, James thinks the philosophical enterprise is most
profoundly assessable in moral terms. Ultimately, the
point of philosophy is to clarify the individual's place in
the world in order to enrich the possibilities for human
fulfillment.

This conception of the moral import of philosophy
sets the basis for James's views on philosophical
method, and for his theory of meaning. Philosophy
must be relevant and useful for life, James holds. It
must be applicable at all points to the concrete empirical particulars of our daily existence. At the outset, as
James introduces the doctrine of pragmatism, he sets
out his view of the ground rules which must be fol-
lowed by any meaningful philosophy:

> There can *be* no difference anywhere that doesn't *make* a
> difference elsewhere—no difference in abstract truth that
> doesn't express itself in a difference in concrete fact and
> in conduct consequent upon that fact, imposed on some-
> body, somehow, somewhere, and somewhen. The whole
> function of philosophy ought to be to find out what de-
> finite difference it will make to you and me, at definite

instants of our life, if this world-formula or that world-formula be the true one.[4]

With this injunction as the cornerstone of his pragmatism, James proposes to subject every philosophical position to the test of practical relevance. The locus of meaning is the interested, goal-positing person, for whom it is required that beliefs have concrete consequences if they are to have a functional role in his life. If a philosophical claim or system has no conceivable consequences in the lives of those who believe in it, then it must count as pragmatically meaningless, from James's point of view. He sees philosophy not as a static set of fixed doctrines, to be contemplated as finished pieces of mental architecture, reflecting eternal principles and realities. He finds abstract a priori philosophical systems, no matter how seemingly profound, to be a denigration of the philosophical ideal—for they do not "touch down" in real life and thus can have no relevance to the fulfillment of human ends. "In this real world of sweat and dirt," James remarks in *Pragmatism*, "it seems to me that when a view of things is 'noble,' that ought to count as a presumption against its truth, and as a philosophic disqualification." [5]

Indeed, it is not only the philosophy of grand deductive systems which falls away as inadequate from James's point of view. He rejects any idea of philosophy which restricts its task exclusively to conceptual analysis. While James accepts the value of logical and conceptual considerations, he thinks philosophy must go beyond this. For insofar as any given philosophical analysis is purely analytic and applicable to any possible world, to that extent it fails to capture the rich particulars unique to our own. As such, from James's point of view, it is incomplete.[6]

It is in the context of his practical conception of philosophy that James propounds the guiding methodological principle of his pragmatism—I shall call it his "principle of experience"—namely, that philosophical inquiry is appropriately restricted to issues which are analyzable in terms of actual or possible experiences. If philosophy ultimately has a practical function, then philosophers must eliminate from their theories any concepts or hypotheses which have no experiential implications or effects. For if there existed a phenomenon which was utterly "transexperiential" or "transempirical"—for which we could imagine no conceivable concrete expressions—then from a practical point of view it would count as nothing at all.[7]

This may look as though James is narrowly positivistic in restricting philosophy to experience, but in fact he is not. In his theory of pragmatic meaning, as we shall see, he articulates quite a broad conception of what kinds of propositions are to count as having experiential implications. Thus, propositions concerning God's goodness, for example, are considered by James to be philosophically legitimate and important.[8]

While James does not draw a narrow band around legitimate philosophizing on the basis of any restrictive criterion of sensory verifiability, he is nevertheless motivated, in what might best be seen as a moral program, to rid philosophy of what he considers to be empty and wasteful discussion. For each major philosophical question he addresses, James uses his principle of experience to clear up the philosophic field. From the pragmatic point of view, James claims, any phenomenon is what it is "known-as," and thus it is senseless to posit the existence of something that is utterly incapable of being experienced and interpreted. The end result, though not positivistic, nevertheless may fairly be called a species of reductionism. For any significant purposes, James holds, the character of any phenomenon is circumscribed by the limits of our possible interpretation of it. The result is that conceptual or logical questions about the nature of a phenomenon are reducible to epistemological questions about what we can know or say about it. Throughout the course of this book we shall examine the way in which James implements this principle. Whatever may be its advantages, there is little doubt that it also carries with it some problematic implications, which we shall have the opportunity to consider.

James's teleological conception of human nature, along with his methodological commitment to the principle of experience, are the main pillars of his pragmatism. But what precisely is James's pragmatism? For a philosophy whose avowed aim is to clarify philosophical issues, the question of the meaning of pragmatism itself is left surprisingly obscure. Like the attitude most philosophers have toward philosophy itself, James was more interested in "doing pragmatism" than in defining it. When he does provide an explicit characterization of what pragmatism stands for, his favorite formulation is that "pragmatism" designates nothing more than a method of doing philosophy, making no substantive points on its own. It is, he asserts, a method for determining the meaning of claims by tracing their practical consequences.[9] James clarifies his doctrine by borrowing a metaphor from the Italian pragmatist Papini. Pragmatism is like a corridor in a hotel, leading to many different rooms. In each room a different sort of philosophy may be promulgated—theism or atheism, idealism or positivism, for example—but in each case if the philosophy is to be meaningful the pragmatic method must be utilized.[10]

Elsewhere, James goes beyond thinking of pragmatism as merely a method which is substantively neutral, and contends that the pragmatic method is more compatible with some sorts of epistemological and metaphysical theories than it is with others. Thus he holds that pragmatism leads naturally to a metaphysical pluralism[11] and to a specific theory of truth.[12]

Perhaps the most popular conception of James's pragmatism revolves around its emphasis, or supposed emphasis, on the primacy of action—action, moreover, at the expense of thought. When James introduces the term "pragmatism" he says it is derived from the "Greek word πράγμα, meaning action, from which our words 'practice' and 'practical' come."[13] He claims elsewhere that "behavior is the aim and end of every sound philosophy," [14] and there are numerous other occasions where James gives the appearance of denigrating or at least de-emphasizing intellectual pursuits and ideals. He appears to substitute a picture of human beings as being narrowly impelled toward the fulfillment of their biological and practical ends. Thus when James asks in the midst of a theological discussion, "Now in which one of us practical Americans here assembled does this conglomeration of attributes [of the divinity] awaken any sense of reality?," [15] and when he analyzes truth in terms of an idea's "cash value," [16] he reinforces an image of his philosophy as narrowly utilitarian and reductionistic, if not crass. An overemphasis on these sorts of remarks in James on the part of some readers, along with some simplistic interpretations of the ideas of other pragmatists as well, have tended to give pragmatism rather a bad name in the popular mind. It has been seen as a philosophy which denigrates intellectual pursuits, indeed, one which denigrates thought; a philosophy of expediency, which posits as the ultimate good actions aimed toward the fulfillment of narrowly egocentric and materialistic ends. "Pragmatic" considerations have been thought to be opposed to considerations of principle, and James's pragmatic philosophy has been seen as the embodiment of American competitiveness, aggressiveness, and materialism.

We shall see in the course of this book just how false a caricature this is. Indeed James overstates his philosophy all too frequently, and there are occasions where he is cavalier in the preeminence he ascribes to actions over thought. Nevertheless, the idea of action per se is not the central notion in his pragmatism. When emphasizing the practical import of ideas, James's most considered intention is not to relate ideas to practice, narrowly conceived. Rather, "practical" activity is understood by James to be activity with a purpose, and in the notion of purpose lies the real meaning of his philosophy.[17] Aims, ideals, ends, the fulfillment of goals: the conative, striving human being is the hub from which James's world-view emanates and develops. His pragmatism is that philosophy which interprets traditional metaphysical, epistemological, and ethical questions in light of their relevance to these human ends. But there is no reason whatever to consider such purposes anti-theoretical, or to think that their fulfillment lies in the performance of actions in any narrow anti-intellectual sense. It is as much a concrete purpose to solve the four-color map problem, say, or to write a perfect sonnet, as it is to search for food.

Following upon James's emphasis on the purposive character of thought is another important meaning that he gives to the notion of the practical. James holds that the fulfillment of purposes can be achieved only in the context of dealing with *particular* facts and events. Thus, in referring to the practical consequences of philosophical claims, he intends to identify their *particular* consequences for our experience and behavior.[18]

James presents his pragmatism as a revolution in philosophy—a shift in philosophical perspective and a revitalization of the philosophic enterprise. If it is to be a meaningful activity, James proclaims, "the centre of gravity of philosophy must . . . alter its place." [19] The emphasis shifts from technical, entirely abstract questions that may be handled in purely logical ways, to questions that must show their pertinence and import for the individual's life. The philosophical enterprise is born out of the concrete conditions of life and ultimately is responsible for referring back to them. Doing philosophy provides no special intellectual refuge, but, like any other activity in which human beings engage, it is susceptible to evaluation in terms of its adequacy for meeting our interests and needs.

In summarizing the major principles of James's pragmatism, we find that it is a practical philosophy, in the sense that it requires of any philosophical point of view that it answer to a real interest. It is based on a conception of the person as purposive and interested in character, whose intellect is used as a tool for the fulfillment of particular ends. The operating methodological principle of James's philosophy is his principle of experience, which functions as a rallying call away from philosophical abstractions and which represents a commitment to solving philosophical problems by reference exclusively to the concrete facts of human life.

James is consistently loyal to these principles in every aspect of his pragmatism. In his ethical theory, for example, he denies the possibility of any transempirical foundation of morality, any transcendent moral order existing independently of felt values. He sees it as his task to account for moral value exclusively within the parameters of concrete experience. This, conjoined with his conception of human beings as volitional and teleological, leads him to the view that moral value is determined by the fulfillment of interests and goals or, as he puts it, that the essence of good is the satisfaction of demand. In a position reminiscent of John Stuart Mill's famous claim that the only way we can tell that something is desirable is if someone actually desires it,[20] James attempts to place moral value on a naturalistic foundation by arguing that, all other things being equal, the fact that something is demanded (in the specific sense of "demand" he has in mind) is sufficient to make it good.

The idea of the interested, teleological, committed individual also provides the basis for James's defense of non-rational grounds for belief. In his doctrine of "the will to believe," by far one of the most controversial parts of his philosophy, James rejects traditionally accepted canons of epistemological reasonableness. He argues, at first sight paradoxically, that there are occasions where it is more reasonable for a person to follow emotional or spiritual reasons for holding a belief—for the sake of fulfilling his hopes, desires, aims, needs, and the like—than it is to believe on more narrowly "rational" grounds. He is the first to grant that objectivity, impartiality, and the judicious assessment of evidence have an important place in human life. Still, his point is that human interests and commitments extend beyond the limits of a disinterested intellect, and he holds that justification of belief must take into account the total context in which the beliefs are formulated and in which they work.

James's theory of truth is perhaps the most famous part of his philosophy, and it is without doubt the most sophisticated embodiment of his pragmatism. Here James's commitment to his principle of experience conjoins with his emphasis on the fulfillment of human interests, to provide the elements of an integrated theory. James insists that it is meaningless to postulate a standing truth between propositions and reality which obtains independently of its being known by human subjects. There is no such thing as truth outside the context of judgments of truth, James maintains, and these judgments are made and justified on the basis of our experience of the world as we know it. From a pragmatic point of view, then, the question of the meaning of truth is reduced to the question of the criteria by which beliefs are justified.

But what are the criteria of justification? Here James comes to the fullest expression of his pragmatism. He holds that since beliefs are tools whose function it is to enable the believer in a given empirical environment to fulfill his purposes and answer his interests, a belief is justified—and hence pragmatically true—if it successfully fulfills this function; that is to say, if it enables the believer to account for and predict his experience in ways that most satisfactorily fulfill his ends.

This conclusion represents a startling reorientation in epistemology, in that James repudiates the commonly accepted view that true beliefs provide a value-free, descriptive representation of reality, unaffected by personl desires or aims. Since from James's point of view, truth is determined by the satisfaction of the believer's purposes and interests, it is ultimately a moral category in his philosophy. The person can no longer be seen as a passive spectator of reality, gathering value-free truths. On James's philosophy human purpose and interest are inexpungibly part of the cognitive situation.

Such a constructionalist and value-laden theory of

truth would hardly be acceptable if one held the view that reality—the object of true beliefs—is something set against the subject as utterly external and objective, uninfluenced by human interpretation and interest. But, as might be expected, James's conception of reality, at least if we are talking about the reality of common-sense physical objects, is no less radically pragmatic than his theory of truth. James will not consider any reality that exists separate from and independently of experience. But the flux of experience provides the basis for many alternative realities, and the common-sense world of physical objects as we know it is just one alternative among many. It is in large part a human construction, and its character is determined by the aims and goals that the various alternative interpretations of experience serve. From a pragmatic point of view, then, reality is a reflection of pragmatic truth, and physical objects as we know them are embodiments of human values.

In *Essays in Radical Empiricism,* James moves the focus of his interest away from the question of pragmatic realities and attempts to construct a metaphysical system in the traditional sense. Here James concerns himself with the ultimate reality—that which provides the grounding for the pragmatically constructed realities of our everyday world. This represents a major shift in philosophical perspective for James. In his pragmatic writings, primarily *Pragmatism* and *The Meaning of Truth,* his "principle of experience" functions as a methodological and epistemological principle restricting the range of legitimate philosophical discourse. James tends to treat "experience" in a mentalistic way, as constituting the psychological data that the subject interprets in the process of constructing pragmatic realities. In James's metaphysical system, which he calls "radical empiricism," "experience" is given a much less subjective cast, and James's "principle of experience" becomes a metaphysical principle in the fullest sense. Experience is raised to the status of being the ultimate and only reality.

Leaving aside for the moment James's radical empiricism, if we look at his pragmatic philosophy as a whole, we find him to be consistent in his orientation and concerns. Whether doing pragmatic metaphysics, ethics, or epistemology, James renders his analyses in terms of the purposive human subject dealing with the world as he understands it. His is paramountly an optimistic and moralistic philosophy. Human thought has a creative and originative function. Facts are humanized and value-laden: reality and truth are based on human ends. The world is plastic and malleable, and there is room for the affirmation and fulfillment of our hopes and faiths. Since the ultimate aim of thought is to create constructively the most propitious context for fulfillment of our ideals and ends, our power is considerable and our mission is profoundly moral.

While James enjoys the advantages of casting his philosophy in such thoroughly humanistic terms, he does not fail to recognize the sorts of problems to which such an approach can lead. For to posit human purpose and desire as the ultimate determinants in such issues as reality, truth, and moral value seems to leave little room for an objective point of view. Indeed, if there is any single most challenging criticism of James's philosophy, it is that his positions are subjectivistic to an unacceptable degree.

In the case of his ethical theory, for example, it is difficult to accept that moral value is determined exclusively by the satisfaction of demand, since it is well-known that human demands may be egocentric, trivial, insensitive, or debased. Regarding his views on the justification of believing on passional grounds, it seems difficult to imagine how a person of intellectual integrity could consider his beliefs justified merely because they answered to his personal needs. James's pragmatic theories of truth and reality are susceptible to the same sort of criticism. If truth depends on what human beings accept as true, given the nature of their experiences and purposes, there seems no guarantee that such "truth" will not be fortuitous or arbitrary. And if physical objects are value-laden constructions, there would appear to be no possibility whatever of an objective world.

James was well aware of the significance of such challenges to his philosophy, and his attempt to meet the requirements of objectivity, while still preserving the distinctive elements of his own point of view, constitutes the center of dramatic tension in his thought. As we shall see, it also remains the source of his greatest difficulty throughout his work. How James attempts to solve these problems, and whether he succeeds, will be a major concern of this book.

2. The Teleology of Mind

OUR OVERVIEW OF JAMES'S philosophy has shown that the teleological subject—with his needs, desires, and interests—plays an indisputably central role in determining the character of the pragmatic world-view. A philosophy that eliminated reference to persons would be relegated to the realm of empty and remote intellectual abstractions having no true pertinence or value. In the present chapter we shall examine closely what James means when he claims that the mind operates teleologically, and we shall consider how he thinks such operations affect the world as we know it. Then we shall move on to consider a complementary view in James's philosophy—that of the relation between thought and action. He holds that in thinking we aim toward the fulfillment of practical ends, and he argues that we fulfill these ends by our actions. But precisely what James means by "action," and precisely what he holds the relation between thought and action to be, are obscure, and as I intend to show, rather confused.

I

Looking first at James's view on the teleological character of mind, we see that his picture of the human being is that of a project-laden, desiring, goal-oriented, purposive, active, interested, value-affirming, interpretive individual, with whatever activity he engages in having as its ultimate aim the fulfillment of his diverse

14

projected ends. It is difficult to find one single term to refer to these goals, desires, purposes, ideals, preferences, wants, and needs. As a general term to refer to all these, James occasionally uses the term "demands." [1] Most prevalently, however, he calls them "interests." [2] Accordingly, I shall use the term "interests" to refer to any of these different embodiments of our volitional, teleological consciousness.

In examining more closely the way a person's interests permeate his understanding of the world, the first point to note is that, on James's view, human cognition is but an aspect or stage of a larger process—a process known as the "reflex arc." The reflex-arc theory, widely accepted during James's time, is designed to explain the activity of the human organism in its relation with the external world. The reflex arc is a triadic process, physiologically based, wherein none of the three stages can occur independently of the other two. It follows this course: sensation, thought, and action. First, the individual is barraged with sensations, some of which he attends to and some of which he ignores. Second, the individual organizes his sensible experiences by categorizing them in certain ways and formulating beliefs about them—this is the cognitional stage of the reflex arc. Finally, on the basis of his understanding, the individual acts in certain ways. [3] This final stage of action is of greatest importance on James's view, since it is by means of action that the individual actually fulfills his interests, and the aim or end of the reflex-arc process is the fulfillment of these practical ends. Interests play a role at every stage, however: they determine which sensations will be attended to; they help determine which categories will be used to interpret, arrange, and explain the sensations; and finally, they influence how the individual will act. We shall consider the stages of the reflex arc in turn, and look more closely at how interest affects each of them.

Given a continuous sensory influx, in James's well-known phrase, a "buzzing, blooming, confusion," the individual attends to certain sensations and ignores

others. Beginning with the very identification of the
material that is to be thought about and understood,
human interest functions to isolate from a large set of
available data those experiences that will be the object
of the individual's thought.[4] James gives a convincing
account of this process in "Reflex Action and Theism."
He asks the members of his audience to attend to all of
the experiences they are presently having, exercising
no selective attention. The result—the flux of uninter-
preted experience—is chaos:

> The strains of my voice, the lights and shades inside the
> room and out, the murmur of the wind, the ticking of the
> clock, the various organic feelings you may happen indi-
> vidually to possess, do these make a whole at all?[5]

James argues that they do not make an intelligible
whole. There is nothing meaningful in the mere fact
that experiences are contemporaneous. In order to
construct a comprehensible picture out of the brute
chaos of incoming sensation, it is up to the individual
to select certain of his experiences and disregard
others, and to associate the selected experiences with
other experiences he has had in the past. Human interest provides the mechanism for attending to and organizing our experience. We interpret our experience
in ways which we find interesting and fruitful, in ways
which answer to our needs, and which are relevant to
our purposes. The audience ignores the sounds of the
ticking of the clock and attends to James's lecture. The
lecture is understood because it evokes associations
with experiences previously had by the audience, experiences the memory of which are retained because
they carry a measure of interest, experiences that are
used to structure and understand presently incoming
data. The principle of selection and organization is
supplied by the subject.

The implications of James's position are extensive.
Interest and selective attention help determine the
identity and meaning not merely of such intangible
phenomena as philosophical lectures. The status of
physical objects is no different:

Helmholtz says that we notice only those sensations which are signs to us of *things*. But what are things? Nothing, as we shall abundantly see, but special groups of sensible qualities, which happen practically or aesthetically to interest us, to which we therefore give substantive names, and which we exalt to this exclusive status of independence and dignity.[6]

This is a striking claim—more striking perhaps when seen less as a claim about the psychology of perception than as a notion about the reality of the physical world. In Chapter 7 we shall consider James's views about the reality and independence of the external world. Here what is important to note is the tremendous weight placed upon human interest in the organization of experience.

After the use of selective attention and the discrimination of objects, the next step occurs when the mind selects again, once more on the basis of interest, which qualities of an object to consider essential to it, and which to consider accidental. The essential qualities of something are taken to be its "real" attributes, the object as it truly is. Its accidental qualities, on the other hand, are those attributes that vary according to the perspective of the perceiver. James argues that it is we who distinguish among them on subjective, aesthetic grounds. A round penny, indeed, looks elliptical in most of the circumstances under which we perceive it, yet we consider its elliptical appearance as failing to represent its true shape. But had our interests been different, James maintains, we may well have chosen to consider the elliptical appearance of the penny to represent its essential shape, and have considered the fact that the penny looks round under certain conditions to be the product of a perspectival view.[7]

This is an interesting position, but is it merely "for aesthetic reasons of my own," [8] as James claims, that I consider certain qualities of objects essential and others accidental? It would seem not. If, in considering ellipticity to be the true shape of the penny, I mean that the penny *really is* elliptical—even though it *looks* round under some circumstances (when seen head-on)—then some curious consequences follow. On the conditions under which the elliptical penny appears round, I would be faced with an object reflecting light from a circumference of points equidistant from its center, in spite of the fact that the points constituting the circumference of this object—because it is elliptical—are not themselves all equidistant from the center. This would leave some points in an inexplicably non-reflective and invisible state.[9] Thus, considering a penny to be an elliptical object that merely looks round when viewed head-on would require more than a different emphasis on my part. It would require serious changes in the laws of optics. Additionally, it is not only how shapes *appear* to us which is important. We rely on things actually *being* one shape rather than another. The laws of aerodynamics require a certain shape to an aircraft's wings, no matter how they look to us from where we sit in the aircraft.

Perhaps this is not what James has in mind. He more likely means something like this: An object has no properties by which it represents itself to us more truly than any others. The penny, as perceived, is not in itself either "really" round or "really" elliptical. We may, if we choose, call the penny "really" elliptical, if one of the things we mean by this is that when viewed head-on the penny appears circular. With equal plausibility, we may call the penny "really" round, if one of the things we mean by this is that when viewed at an angle the penny appears elliptical. We do not, by naming an object one way rather than another, necessarily commit ourselves to different expectations as to how that object will behave; though by so doing we may show that our attention is focused on one property of the object rather than another.

If this is James's intention in this passage, then his point is merely a linguistic one. Since there is no one essential shape of the penny as perceived, various alternative ways of characterizing the shape of the penny may each be correct. To call James's point linguistic is not to deny that it may embody considerable insight about the psychology of naming and its implications for practical life. It is only to deny that any empirical consequences involving the objects we name follow from the names we give to them.

It is worth noting that when James contends that interests affect how we shall differentiate our perceptions into things, and influence as well which qualities of things we shall consider essential to them, he is careful to delineate the extent to which the subject himself is responsible for making such determinations. He does not consider each individual percipient to be in an isolated position of interpreting the world de novo, building from the basis of his sensorium and diverse interests a conceptual scheme, and on the basis of that, a world of particular objects. While it is true that the individual does have considerable power and range in interpreting his experience, it is also true that human experience as interpreted exhibits much in the way of shared similarities which cross the boundaries of time, space, language, and even personal interests:

> The human race as a whole largely agrees as to what it shall notice and name, and what not. And among the noticed parts we select in much the same way for accentuation and preference or subordination and dislike.[10]

The fact that we have many common interests goes some way to explain the fact that we construct similar interpretations of the flux of experience. A deeper reason, however, from James's point of view, lies in the fact that we share "common-sense categories" including such notions as reality, causality, mind, and body. In different books, James gives different explanations of the genesis of these categories. In *Pragmatism* he suggests that they are embedded in our language.[11] In *The Principles of Psychology* he argues that they are embodied in the structure of our brains.[12] But in either case, James sees them as a priori, and common to us all.[13]

There is considerably more to be said on James's

view of the way in which the individual interprets his experience, and we will return to this issue in Chapter 7. To conclude our examination at this point, we may summarize James's view briefly as follows. The individual is barraged with a flux of sensations. In order to make sense of that disorganized jumble of experiences, he must provide his own structure, and he does this by means of selective attention and the application of interpretive categories. He must ignore some incoming sensations, give special attention to others, and relate sensations which are temporally non-contiguous, in order to arrive at a workable understanding of the world as he experiences it. The individual's interests provide the criterion in terms of which this process is enacted. His interpretation of his experience contains much that is not particular to him alone. What he attends to and emphasizes is determined to an extent by categories of interpretation, shared in common with others. Within that common conceptual scheme, however, there is much play for the individual's own particular interests to determine how he will select from the stream of experience and arrive at an acceptable interpretation of the world.

II

Cognition operates as part of a systematic process. As such, it requires supplementation. If thinking is to function in its role of fulfilling the purposes of the thinker, if it is to answer his interests, meet his needs, etc., there must be some mechanism whereby these results can be achieved. On James's scheme, that mechanism is action. As the final stage in the reflex arc, action is designed to fulfill the thinker's practical ends. As such, on James's conception, action is intimately related to thought.

While James has much to say about thought, action, and the relation between them, his writings fall short of providing a fully elaborated and consistent position. As we shall see, James could have done more: first, to specify precisely and consistently what he takes to be the relation between thought and action; and second, to clarify exactly what he means by the term "action" itself. He wavers on what he takes to be designated by the term "action," and it is partly as a result of this that he has several different conceptions of the relation between thought and action.

As we have already observed, James's idea of the relation between thought and action is that thinking is part of a larger reflexive and fundamentally volitional activity. The importance and value of thinking consist solely in their contribution to the realization or fulfillment of practical ends, and these results are attained by means of action. "The possession of true thoughts means everywhere the possession of invaluable instruments of action. . . ." [14] "The idea is thus, when functionally considered, an instrument for enabling us the better to *have to do* with the object and to act about it." [15] "What characterizes both consent and belief is the cessation of theoretic agitation. . . . When this is the case, motor effects are apt to follow." [16] These remarks are characteristic. Perhaps the most detailed description of the role of action in the reflex arc is provided in "Reflex Action and Theism":

> The structural unit of the nervous system is in fact a triad, neither of whose elements has any independent existence. The sensory impression exists only for the sake of awaking the central process of reflection, and the central process of reflection exists only for the sake of calling forth the final act. All action is thus *re*-action upon the outer world; and the middle stage of consideration or contemplation or thinking is only a place of transit, the bottom of a loop, both whose ends have their point of application in the outer world. *If it should ever have no roots in the outer world, if it should ever happen that it led to no active measures, it would fail of its essential function, and would have to be considered either pathological or abortive.* The current of life which runs in at our eyes or ears is meant to run out at our hands,

feet, or lips. The only use of the thoughts it occasions while inside is to determine its direction to whichever of these organs shall, on the whole, under the circumstances actually present, act in the way most propitious to our welfare.[17]

It should be noted at the outset that in these passages, and others like them, James makes no distinction between mere bodily movements and actions properly so-called. If an action may be described as an instance of characteristically intelligent and purposive behavior, performed by an agent, then actions are not the same thing as mere bodily movements, and the two ought to be kept distinct. Automatic reflex movements, muscle spasms, and the like, are clearly bodily movements, but they do not qualify as actions in the proper sense of that term. This point is important because, as we shall see, it is part of a complex set of distinctions which would have been helpful, but which James neglected to make.

On the reflex-arc model as James articulates it, the value of a thought is measured primarily, if not exclusively, in terms of the propitiousness of the actions that are generated by it. If the reflex arc is arrested at the cognitional stage, then something has gone awry. If an instance of thinking does not lead to action, then that thinking is, in James's terms, either "pathological" or "abortive." Whatever the exact meaning James may have attached to these terms, it is clear that he views thoughts which do not lead to action to be deficient in certain respects. Thinking naturally and directly leads to action, James holds, and cognitive activity that does not lead to these results has somehow broken down.

Yet this position seems quite difficult to maintain. Insofar as James is using the notion of action as minimally involving some form of overt bodily movement, then his position seems clearly false. For we sometimes think normally, fruitfully, and extensively, without our ideas resulting in any kind of action whatever. Considering the structure of a symphony, interpreting the meaning of the Trojan War, and contemplating the problem of evil, for example, are all instances of legitimate cognitive activity. While these thoughts may lead to action under some conceivable circumstances, they usually do not do so. And the evident fact that they need not do so is sufficient to falsify James's theory.

This point is certainly clear enough, and the problem is merely that James overstates his own case in the passages we have cited. He is not unaware of the possibility, indeed likelihood, of there being perfectly acceptable (non-deficient) instances of cognitive activity that lead only to deferred action or establish only a tendency to act—a tendency that may in fact never be actualized. Indeed, in a number of discussions concerning the relation between thought and action, particularly in his psychological works, James makes it quite clear that he takes that relation to be a dispositional one. On this version of James's view, he claims that while thought *naturally* leads to action, it need not *invariably* do so. The action to which a thought on its own would invariably lead may be performed belatedly, or never be performed at all, if that particular thought-action sequence is inhibited by another thought establishing a contrary tendency to act.[18] Thus, for example, taken by itself the individual's belief that the room is too warm would lead him to open the window. But he may not in fact open it if he thought that to do so would be to let in the street noise, and thereby interrupt his work.

On this dispositional account, James still may be said to be using the reflex-arc model to explain the import and function of cognitive activity, and to set out the relation between thought and action. It is just that the picture is more complicated than it heretofore appeared. Rather than understanding any particular action in terms of a singly occurring reflex arc, we can best understand most of the individual's behavior as the result that prevails when a number of conflicting tendencies to act, based on different psychological states, exert pressure against one another. To sum up, what first appeared to be a direct causal link between a particular thought and a specific piece of behavior, becomes, on this more sophisticated version of James's view, a matter of each thought establishing only a disposition to act in a certain way.

This dispositional analysis of the relation between thought and action is far more plausible than the claim that thinking leads to action invariably and directly. It does not yet seem fully adequate, however, for it seems quite clear that some ideas do not establish even as much as a tendency to act on the part of the believer. While a literary critic, for instance, might find that his contemplation of the character of Hamlet established in him a disposition to act in some way—to write a book perhaps—it may be that no tendency to act whatsoever is established in other persons thinking on the same topic. Similarly, an astronomer may be inclined to act on his belief that there are planets in other galaxies, for example by involving himself in various experiments should the opportunity arise; but most persons, sharing that same belief, would not be inclined to act on it in any way at all.

Both of the alternatives regarding the relation between thought and action which we have considered thus far involve the notion of the individual engaging in some sort of bodily movement as part of what it means for him to perform an action. Given bodily movement as a requirement for action, there appears to be no invariable relation between thought and action, or even between thought and the disposition to act. Perhaps the way to sustain the view that thought invariably either leads to action or establishes a disposition to act is to eliminate entirely overt bodily movement as a requirement for action. This is the alternative James chooses:

> You must remember that, when I talk of action here, I mean action in the widest sense. I mean speech, I mean writing, I mean yeses and noes, and tendencies "from"

things and tendencies "toward" things, and emotional determinations; and I mean them in the future as well as in the immediate present.[19]

James's view of action is drawn to its ultimate point when he contends that refraining from acting may itself be an act. Characterizing the individual's behavior as "including every possible sort of fit reaction on the circumstances into which he may find himself brought by the vicissitudes of life," [20] James claims:

> *Not* to speak, *not* to move, is one of the most important of our duties, in certain practical emergencies. "Thou shalt refrain, renounce, abstain!" This often requires a great effort of will power, and, physiologically considered, is just as positive a nerve function as is motor discharge.[21]

There is an important insight in James's observation that there are occasions when refraining from speaking or moving may be considered actions. We may indeed, as James observes, exercise will power—in fact to a considerable degree—in refraining from doing certain things; and exercising abstinence or restraint in certain contexts may accurately be called doing something, or acting, in a legitimate sense of the word. When someone keeps from violently expressing his anger, goes on a fast, or stops smoking, for example, it is certainly reasonable to characterize him as doing something, indeed, as doing something which may be quite difficult. Yet in recognizing performances such as these to be actions, James would have been more clear-sighted had he made more of his observation that such doings often require the exercise of self-control, determination, or the like. Instead, in the remarks we have cited, James considers a sufficient condition of the performance of an action to be the occurrence in the individual of activity in the nervous system.

In some instances James uses a physiological rather than a neurological criterion. He appears to be willing to substitute any physiological activity, no matter how minute, for "action" as it is ordinarily understood. In the following passage, thought need not result in action in any ordinarily recognizable sense, or even in overt bodily movement. The occurrence of a mere physiological change is sufficient for the reflex arc to have been completed:

> The fact is that there is no sort of consciousness whatever, be it sensation, feeling, or idea, which does not directly and of itself tend to discharge into some motor effect. The motor effect need not always be an outward stroke of behavior. It may be only an alteration of the heart-beats or breathing, or a modification in the distribution of blood, such as blushing or turning pale; or else a secretion of tears, or what not. But, in any case, it is there in some shape when any consciousness is there; and a belief as fundamental as any in modern psychology is the belief at last attained that conscious processes of any sort, conscious processes merely as such, *must* pass over into motion, open or concealed.[22]

Whatever happened to actions? In any ordinary sense, they seem to have disappeared. It now appears evident that the reflex-arc theory commits James only to the true but rather uninteresting point that whenever a thought occurs, some neurological or physiological change in the organism is bound to result. But this tells us very little. Clearly, the fact that these sorts of changes occur in a person is, if not irrelevant, at least not sufficient for the performance of an action by that person.[23] In short, James seems to have forsaken entirely the integrity of the notion of action.

Aside from the philosophical difficulties involved in reducing actions to physiological or neurological changes, such a conception of action in any case would fail to provide James with what he hopes to gain from the reflex-arc theory. The pragmatic emphasis on the active goal-fulfilling agent is of systematic importance in James's philosophy. Thinking is designed to fulfill human interests, and actions are the means by which this is achieved. But if the actions to which James refers need be no more than changes in synapses or glands, if "action" may be no more than increased heartbeat, then it is difficult to see how such "actions" could fulfill any but the most insignificant interests. Given the role James requires of action, it would seem that he should restrict this term to refer only to behavior of a significant and potentially useful sort.

In summing up our analysis of James's theory, we must conclude that he leaves us with many unresolved problems. First, he is not sufficiently clear on the question of the relation between thought and action — claiming in some instances that thought establishes only a disposition to act, and elsewhere that it leads to action immediately and directly. Second, when he analyzes the relation between thought and action, he fails to differentiate between actions properly so-called, mere bodily movements, and minute physiological or neurological changes.[24]

The critical question is: Why is James so all-embracing about what is to count as an action? Why, in particular, does he consider it acceptable to count merely neurological or physiological changes as actions? One reason may be that he was forced to this position in his attempt to defend his theory about the relationship between thought and action. It may have been that, unwilling to renounce his position that thought does result in action, and having to account for obvious counterexamples, James chose to broaden his conception of action to include these small bodily changes. The neurological/physiological criterion gives James a way to consider such phenomena as changes in attitude, emotions, preferences, or expectations to be actions; to use his own language — "yeses and noes, and tendencies 'from' things and tendencies 'toward' things, and emotional determinations."

A second and more important reason is this: James would find it appropriate to define the notion of "action" quite broadly due to his conception of the volitional nature of consciousness. When James considers "yeses," "noes," and other volitional, intentional, and affective states to be actions, he is, albeit inaccurately, making an important point. He is bringing to our attention the fact that these states are akin to actions in a number of important ways. To change one's attitude, for example, is characteristically to engage oneself with the world in a new way. To realign one's expectations is to take a stand, commit oneself, if even in very small degree, to the reality of a different future. The changes with which James is concerned here help determine the character of the individual as a dynamic, goal-oriented, energetic source and center of activity and change. Of paramount importance is the fact that these committed states affect practical future consequences in the individual's life; and insofar as they affect the individual's future, they help determine whether his interests will be fulfilled. These commitments are full-fledged responses and may well have full-fledged effects. Insofar as these volitional states have the same effects on the individual's life as actions proper, they may be seen as pragmatically identical to actions in the relevant respects.

To sum up our discussion in this chapter, we find that the individual's interests are involved at every stage of the reflex arc—perceiving, thinking, and acting. The aim of cognition is not to reflect a preexistent reality, but rather to provide the individual with the richest, fullest, and most fruitful way of understanding his experiences and dealing with them.[25] The success of a cognitive operation is to be judged in terms of the contribution the thinking makes to the success or well being of the individual's life overall—and this is a matter of fulfilling multitudinous and diverse goals. The exercise of our intellectual and cognitive capacities is important, not because such capacities are intrinsically valuable, but rather because the intellect is the best instrument we have for answering our interests, whatever these may be.

As we shall see more fully in Chapter 7, James's account of the function of thought constitutes an unambiguous rejection of the traditional conception of cognition as properly a disinterested activity in which persons engage for the sake of knowing an independent and objective reality. James's aim is to reject the traditional "intellectualist" assumption, apparent throughout the history of philosophy in various guises and forms, that thinking at its best is a purely theoretical activity, and that the function of mind is fundamentally rational. On the contrary, for James, cognition is a dynamic and practical enterprise. James's model of the knowing process pictures the person as contributing to the reality, unfinished without him, which he simultaneously seeks to know.[26] The individual does this, as we have seen, by selectively attending to his experience, by contributing categorial interpretations, and by acting in appropriate ways. The selection, interpretation, and utilization of experiential data are, as we have seen, determined by the subject's interests.

James's invocation of subjective preference in his analysis of the cognitive process places the consciousness of the thinker in the position of being the ultimate criterion of the adequacy of ideas. On James's account, the epistemological emphasis moves on to the thinker himself as the pivotal and important point.[27] Epistemological assessment is ultimately a practical, value-laden one. The most salient criterion of cognitive value is the fulfillment of subjective preference.

3. The Concept of Pragmatic Meaning

WE HAVE NOW SEEN that for James, the mind is a teleological mechanism. On his view thinking is only a
stage in a larger process, the reflex arc, whose natural
end-point is action. Ideas and beliefs are tools whose
function is to benefit the thinker in the concrete situations of his life—to help him fulfill his goals in the context of empirical obstacles and constraints. On James's
view the role of thinking is to redirect the individual
into experience, better prepared to meet future contingencies.[1] It follows from this that intellectual activity,
if it is to perform its function, must have consequences
outside itself for feeling and conduct. It is from this
position that James rejects traditional philosophical
attitudes toward thinking as an activity that is self-
contained and valuable in itself. James's theory of
meaning develops from these ideas. For James, to call a
belief or idea meaningful is to recognize it as fulfilling
its function. But if this is the case, then meaning must
be integrally tied to the thinker's concrete or practical
concerns. James is not interested in meanings as isolated from experience and conduct—indeed he considers this topic unworthy of serious concern. To
search for the meaning of ideas independently of their
applications and·functions would be like trying to
understand the nature of a tool without inquiring
about what it can be used to do.

In centering meaning on the function and application of ideas and beliefs James steps outside the range of traditional philosophy on this issue. Typically, philosophers have held that the meaning of an idea is one thing, and the way it can be used is quite another; indeed, that meaning must be fully determined before any assessment of function can be made. In this chapter we shall consider James's theory of meaning with two issues in mind. First, we shall look at how James determines which sorts of claims are meaningful, and how he eliminates those which are not. Second, we shall consider the difficult and slippery question as to what James means by "meaning" itself. As we examine the dispute between James and other philosophers over the meaning of beliefs, we shall find that what James means by "meaning" is something different from traditional views on the subject. For James's theory of meaning is a theory of *pragmatic* meaning, and this difference marks a departure from other theories in important ways.

I

It should be noted at the outset that, although James's ideas on meaning are among the most pervasive and important elements of his philosophy, he does not develop his account in any systematic way. Rather, for the most part his ideas on meaning are found embedded in his individual analyses of the meanings of particular philosophical claims. As scholars have recognized, James was most interested in using the pragmatic method to identify the meanings of various puzzling philosophical ideas — "truth," "reality," "God," and "substance," for example. But the meaning of meaning was not itself a question with which he dealt directly in any extensive way.[2] Because of this, an analysis of James's theory presents unusual difficulties and requires a great deal of construction, inference, and interpretation on the part of his commentators. The interpretation to be given here is intended to account for James's numerous remarks on meaning in a way that shows them to embody a single principle — consistent within itself and of a piece with the remainder of his philosophy.

The first question we have to consider concerns the criterion James uses to determine whether an idea or belief is meaningful. Although there has been little agreement among commentators regarding James's position here, the best-known analysis of James's view is given by A. O. Lovejoy. In his essay "The Thirteen Pragmatisms," Lovejoy gives an interpretation of James's theory and develops important criticisms of his position. Lovejoy argues that though James allegedly holds a single theory of meaning, because of an ambiguity in the terms in which the theory is expressed, he actually holds two different theories.[3] Moreover, Lovejoy contends that the criterion for meaningfulness is different on each theory, and that those things considered meaningful according to the first theory are not extensionally equivalent with those considered meaningful according to the second.

On the one hand, Lovejoy contends, James may be understood as holding that the meaning of a proposition is restricted to its "predictive import"—the future experiential consequences to which the proposition points—"consequences which those who accept the proposition *ipso facto* anticipate as experiences that somebody is subsequently to have."[4] This may be described as the "verificationist" aspect of James's theory, and indeed the view does seem very much like the verifiability criterion of meaning as it has appeared in some of its various formulations. On the other hand, Lovejoy argues, James may be understood as holding a theory of meaning that makes the meaning of a proposition consist entirely in the future consequences of *believing* it, independently of whether the proposition itself enables the believer to infer experiential consequences. According to this criterion, anything a person believed would be meaningful if the fact that he believed it had consequences for his life.[5]

Lovejoy contends that these two criteria of meaning are incompatible. On the first criterion, the idealist's claim that "The Absolute exists," for instance, would be meaningless, since no particular empirical consequences follow from the assumption that it is true. On the second criterion, however, this same proposition would be meaningful as long as belief in the Absolute had some effect on the life of the believer — for example, if such a belief were emotionally restorative or morally consoling.

Lovejoy then goes on to add the criticism that each of James's criteria of meaning is in its own way inadequate. He holds that the first criterion circumscribes far too narrowly the range of significant propositions, for it eliminates traditional metaphysical, moral, and other philosophical propositions from the realm of legitimate discourse. If James does hold the first criterion as Lovejoy describes it, then Lovejoy's criticism would appear to be correct. For as the plethora of arguments against various forms of logical positivism have since shown, a criterion of meaning that counts only empirical predictive import as relevant must be considered overly restrictive. Lovejoy considers James's second criterion, on the other hand, to be far too broad. On this criterion meaning is tied to consequences of belief, and if an individual were affected by beliefs that were too vague or confused to be intelligible in any ordinary sense, James would still have to count those beliefs as meaningful. Thus, for example, the belief that "evil is a form of good" might somehow function in an energizing or inspiring way for its believers, and would thus be considered meaningful on James's second criterion, in spite of the fact that it made no literal sense whatsoever.

Lovejoy's analysis of James, and the questions to which it gives rise, are still being addressed in the literature, and there is still no clear agreement as to precisely what James accomplishes in his theory of meaning.[6] Is it true that James inadvertently promulgates two distinct criteria of meaning, and if so, are they incompatible? What exactly is the relationship between predictive import and consequences of belief? The first step toward resolving these questions is to determine whether Lovejoy's initial bifurcation of James's theory is correct. Looking first at the notion of predictive import, we find that it is quite a rich concept in James's theory, involving more than a proposition's empirically verifiable consequences. In fact, on James's view, the predictive import of a proposition may be metaphysical rather than empirical in character. Thus, for instance, the proposition "God exists" can be meaningful on James's predictive-import criterion, for this proposition enables the theist to anticipate a different cosmic future — even though not a different empirical one — from that anticipated by the non-theist (or as James would have it, the "materialist"). From an empirical standpoint, James considers theism and materialism to be equivalent. According to both doctrines, the universe is expected to run itself down in accord with scientific principles, with all human life coming to an end. Thus, as an empirical issue, the debate between materialism and theism is meaningless on his account. But these doctrines nevertheless constitute genuinely meaningful alternatives when they are taken from another point of view. James holds that the genuine and important difference between materialism and theism lies rather in their different *metaphysical* consequences. On the theistic hypothesis, we may expect the preservation and ultimate fulfillment of moral ideals, since God is there to insure it, while on the materialistic hypothesis we may not.[7]

On James's predictive import criterion of meaningfulness, then, a proposition is meaningful only if those who accept it thereby anticipate certain consequences, *either* empirical *or* metaphysical. But if this is the case, then criticisms of James for being narrowly positivistic in what he is willing to count as meaningful are incorrect.[8]

Moving to the second aspect of James's theory, we have seen that Lovejoy interprets James as holding that a proposition is meaningful even if it has no predictive import, as long as consequences follow from believing it. Lovejoy uses as evidence James's discussion of Absolute Idealism in *Pragmatism*, where James claims that "you cannot redescend into the world of particulars by the Absolute's aid, or deduce any necessary consequences of detail important for your life from your idea of his nature." [9] Nevertheless, James contends, belief in the Absolute does have some pragmatic meaning because it provides security and religious comfort for some people. These remarks would seem to give strong support to Lovejoy's interpretation, for James clearly appears to be ignoring the predictive import condition and claiming that consequences of belief by themselves are sufficient to confer meaningfulness on the proposition believed.

While it is true that James's remarks on the consequences of belief, here and in other passages as well, seem reasonably open to this construal, still a close examination of the text will show that he does not intend to count consequences of belief as meaningful in isolation from anything else. The concept of the Absolute is meaningful not because of the consequences of believing it simpliciter. It is meaningful because it has predictive import as well. While this concept is in many respects predictively sterile, there is nevertheless some predictive import to the notion, although it is indefinite. James claims that you cannot "deduce any necessary consequences *of detail* important for your life from your idea of [the Absolute's] nature." [10] One cannot make *specific* experiential predictions from the claim that "The Absolute exists," nor can one make *detailed* inferences about future cosmic events. Yet if it is true that the Absolute exists, then we may anticipate that good will prevail. And it is this expectation that explains and legitimizes certain consequences of belief. It is due to this anticipation that believers in the Absolute derive "religious comfort" from the notion, and feel entitled to give up their moral responsibility. James explains the situation as follows:

What do believers in the Absolute mean by saying that their belief affords them comfort? They mean that since *in the Absolute finite evil is "overruled" already*, we may, therefore, whenever we wish, treat the temporal as if it were potentially the eternal, be sure that we can trust its outcome, and, without sin, dismiss our fear and drop the worry of our finite responsibility.[11]

Clearly, James holds that the consequences of believing in the Absolute are of primary importance here. But rather than separating the consequences of believing from their predictive import, and thereby leaving them unexplained, he sees the two as closely related. The consequences which follow from believing that "the Absolute exists"—the feelings of comfort—derive from that proposition's predictive import—the prediction that good will prevail.

Other examples as well make it evident that James's criterion of meaningfulness includes both predictive import and consequences of belief. Consider, for instance, James's discussion of design in nature. When the concept is taken abstractly, with the believer specifying neither what design nor what designer, then the belief in design is pragmatically meaningless. When the notion is made concrete, however—when, for example, design is seen as the product of a theistic God—then the belief is meaningful:

> Returning with it into experience, we gain a more confiding outlook on the future. If not a blind force but a seeing force runs things, we may reasonably expect better issues.[12]

When in the next sentence James claims that "this vague confidence in the future is the sole pragmatic meaning at present discernible in the terms design and designer," [13] he should not be interpreted as claiming that here consequences of belief by themselves constitute meaning. The notion of having confidence in something involves both an element of prediction and an element of feeling. Having confidence in p is at once expecting certain sorts of events to occur (in this case "we may reasonably expect better issues") and having certain feelings (in this case having feelings of security) which are appropriate to that expectation. Both predictive import and the attendant consequences of belief jointly determine the meaningfulness of the claim that there is design, and together constitute its meaning.

Similarly, in the materialism-theism debate, both predictive import and the consequences of belief are the joint determinants of meaning:

> Materialism means simply the denial that the moral order is eternal, and the cutting off of ultimate hopes; theism means the affirmation of an eternal moral order and the letting loose of hope.[14]

The importance of these examples lies in their showing that James does not have two incompatible criteria, or two divergent conceptions of meaning. While the predictive import of a proposition and the consequences of believing it are logically distinct notions, they nevertheless function inseparably as part of a single principle in James's theory. In sum, James's criterion of meaning can be stated as follows: A proposition believed is meaningful if and only if it has predictive import (however vague) and *thus* is such that concrete consequences follow from believing it.

Such a conclusion is seen to be compelling once James's theory of meaning is understood in the context of his views on the function of thought. These latter views have been virtually ignored in the literature on his theory of meaning; yet it is these that provide the foundation for his criterion of meaningfulness and clarify the relationship in his theory between predictive import and consequences of belief. A proposition is pragmatically meaningful if and only if it is functional to believe; and a belief is functional if and only if it leads the believer into the future differently prepared than he would be if he did not hold it. The individual's belief prepares him for the future by enabling him to make predictions about it, and thus by leading him to

have certain attitudes and emotions, and most importantly, to engage in certain sorts of conduct that are
(relative to his purposes) appropriate to that future as
envisioned. As such, the meaning of a proposition is
determined by the consequences that follow from it,
conjoined with the different attitudes, feelings, and actions in the life of the believer which arise from the fact
that he anticipates those consequences.

II

In James's view, meaning is essentially related to the
individual's practical concerns. With its emphasis on
the practical value of beliefs, James's theory appears to
be considerably different from traditional theories of
meaning, and one may begin to wonder whether in
James's hands the question of meaning itself has become transformed. What kind of meaning is pragmatic
meaning? John Dewey, in outlining what he takes to be
two alternative interpretations of James's analysis, is
one philosopher who questions James's intentions.

> Does Mr. James employ the pragmatic method to discover
> the value in terms of the consequences in life of some
> formula which has its logical content already fixed; or
> does he employ it to criticize and revise and, ultimately, to
> constitute the meaning of that formula?[15]

Dewey's alternatives are instructive, for James's view
appears to be genuinely open to both interpretations.
Is the notion of pragmatic meaning used merely to
specify the value of a belief, independent of its cognitive (or in Dewey's language, its "logical") content, or
does the value of a belief in fact define its cognitive
meaning? On the one hand, almost all major commentators have opted for Dewey's second alternative. They
have taken James to be concerned with the traditional
question of the cognitive meaning or intelligible content of ideas and beliefs. Traditional philosophical
theories of meaning—such as ideational, referential,

and behavioral theories, for example[16]—are all addressed to the issue of cognitive meaning, and it would seem reasonable to expect the same of any philosophical analysis, including James's. Indeed there is good evidence, in a large sample of James's writings, that his analysis is concerned with cognitive meaning. For instance, James frequently alludes to Peirce's pragmatic rule—which determines meaning according to an idea's consequences—and applies this rule (as he understands it) in specific instances.[17] Peirce himself took his pragmatic rule to be a cognitive meaning rule, and thus it would most plausibly be seen as such in James as well. Elsewhere James seems to be pointing to cognitive meaning when he invokes the notion of a "distinct idea" in *Some Problems of Philosophy:*

> If, questioning whether a certain concept be true or false, you can think of absolutely nothing that would practically differ in the two cases, you may assume that the alternative is meaningless and that your concept is no distinct idea.[18]

In *Pragmatism,* we find additional evidence that James is concerned with cognitive meaning. Here James approvingly quotes the chemist Ostwald:

> "In what respects would the world be different if this alternative or that were true? If I can find nothing that would become different, then the alternative has no sense." [19]

If Ostwald holds a pragmatic criterion of meaning, as James contends, then there is good reason to suppose that the pragmatic criterion is meant to be a criterion of cognitive meaning; for to say that a contention "has no sense" is (ordinarily) to say that it is cognitively meaningless.

While these passages support the interpretation of James's theory as an account of cognitive meaning, there is also opposing evidence that appears to favor instead the first alternative posed by Dewey. There are discussions in which James rejects certain philosophical

contentions as meaningless not because he finds them
to be unintelligible, but rather because he considers
them trivial and idle—that is to say, narrowly and
triflingly intellectual. His concern in these passages is to
point out the conditions necessary for serious and responsible inquiry, and he rejects certain debates as
meaningless because he thinks they are not worthy of
pursuit by serious individuals. In *Pragmatism,* for
example, James repudiates those metaphysicians who
dispute about issues having no practical consequences,
not because he thinks their claims are literally nonsen-
sical or conceptually confused, but rather because he
considers their enterprise "but pompous trifling," and
believes that "the endowment of a professorship for
such a being would be silly." [20] In "Philosophical Conceptions and Practical Results," James argues that if this
were the last moment of the world, the debate between
theism and materialism would be meaningless. The
competing doctrines in this context "offer a perfectly
idle and insignificant alternative" because, if there is to
be no future, they can perform no function. The issue
is meaningless under these circumstances, James holds,
because "the problem would be purely intellectual." As
such, the competing claims are not deemed unintelligible, but rather valueless and unimportant. [21]

Given the evidence both for and against interpreting
James's theory as an account of cognitive meaning, it
begins to appear that James himself wanted it both
ways. At times this becomes manifest in the course of a
single discussion. In *The Varieties of Religious Experience,*
for instance, James begins a discussion of God's attributes by invoking Peirce's rule, and by claiming that
the theologians' conceptions of God's metaphysical
attributes are "destitute of all intelligible significance." [22] He goes on to claim, however, not that these
concepts are unintelligible, but only that they are valueless:

> . . . I must frankly confess that even though these attri-
> butes were faultlessly deduced, I cannot conceive of its

being of the smallest consequence to us religiously that any one of them should be true.[23]

This desire to embody both alternatives is shown again in "Philosophical Conceptions," when James is discussing the British empiricists.[24] In describing how Locke eliminates certain conceptions of personal identity as "void of intelligible meaning," James appears to recognize that Locke's criterion is a criterion of cognitive meaning, and he endorses it. As the discussion proceeds, however, James invokes his other notion of meaning. Certain claims are rejected as meaningless because they "never make an appreciable difference to us in action." "And what matters it," James asks, "when all propositions are practically meaningless, which of them be called true or false?" James is not claiming here that these contentions are unintelligible and therefore cannot be assigned a truth-value. He is making the quite different point that their truth or falsity is unimportant.

Another such case appears in *Some Problems of Philosophy*.[25] In a discussion of the meaning of concepts, James differentiates the "substantive content" of a concept from its "functional value," or pragmatic meaning, and he appears to use the notion of substantive content as replaceable for cognitive meaning. He goes on to state that while the substantive content of a concept may be worthy of stationary contemplation, the more important part of its significance is its pragmatic meaning. Shortly thereafter, however, he contends that the sole meaning of a concept is its pragmatic meaning, and denies that the substantive part of a concept is any part of its meaning at all. Pragmatic meaning is first taken as a kind of meaning additional to substantive content or cognitive meaning, and then taken to be a replacement for it.

III

Is pragmatic meaning intended to be identical to cognitive meaning or distinguishable from it? Is James concerned with intelligible content, or with pragmatic effects? It should now be evident that we can make no clear choice between these interpretations of James's philosophy, and we may begin to suspect that each of the alternatives before us fails to capture the true import and originality of his position. The problem in interpreting James derives from the fact that he is using traditional categories in an effort to go beyond them. On the one hand, in his use of the notions of predictive import and consequences of belief, his effort is not to analyze the cognitive meaning of ideas and beliefs, as "cognitive meaning" is ordinarily understood. On the other hand, he does not wish to count predictive import and consequences of belief as separable from meaning in any significant sense. The problem, of course, is that there seems to be no possibility that James can achieve both of these alternatives, and the solution emerges only when we realize that James is introducing a new idea of meaning itself. He is willing to grant that ideas have "cognitive meaning" independently of their consequences, if by this it is meant that concepts partake in logical relations with other concepts, and that their abstract meanings may be articulated in ways which make sense on some level. Yet James does not believe that "cognitive meaning" in this abstract analytic sense captures the true meaning of what we say and think. James's theory of meaning is an attempt to reorient the approach to the problem of meaning in ways that he considers to be more fruitful and more profound, and in his eyes this implies that the nature of meaning itself must be understood pragmatically—in terms of how meanings function in concrete terms for us as cognizing individuals.

Reverting to his views on the function of cognition, we have seen that James holds that the role of mental activity is not to apprehend "meanings" in isolation from conduct, or to be self-sufficing in any way at all. For James, a belief or idea is truly meaningful only if it serves the purposes of cognition. Since these purposes are ultimately practical, the idea of meaning itself becomes transformed to stand for the relevance of the belief or idea to the believer's life. Thus "meaning" in any significant philosophical sense for James is *pragmatic* meaning. The notion of pragmatic meaning does not stand for cognitive meaning as ordinarily understood, for it goes beyond abstract definitions or conceptual equivalences. Nor does it stand merely for the effects that happen to follow contingently upon holding a given belief. Pragmatic meaning involves the ways in which ideas or beliefs can be applied for concrete purposes, under specific empirical conditions, and with specific implications and effects.

James's theory is part of a broader attempt to direct philosophy back into fruitful channels, for he feels that philosophers frequently approach problems in a way that is too abstract, out of touch, and out of phase with the concrete conditions of life. Debates devoted to exclusively logical relationships between abstract ideas make no sense from a pragmatic point of view, and the point of James's criterion of meaning is to discount philosophical concepts that have no experiential implications or consequences, and philosophical disputes that fail to help individuals understand their experiences or act on them. For James, as for Wittgenstein later in the century, the meaning of an idea is not separable from the context of its use. To articulate the meaning of an idea is not to rehearse a list of other logically equivalent ideas; it is to use that idea as a tool in the context of particular concrete problems and concerns. As Wittgenstein was to hold that it is misguided to search for the meaning of a word outside of that word's own language-game, James holds that abstracting concepts out of their particular uses, and treating those abstractions by themselves as significant, are bound to result in sterility and confusion.[26] James's concern is to understand the meaning of ideas *in use,* and this is what he calls pragmatic meaning.

In sum, the pragmatic meaning of a belief or idea is not intended to stand for its cognitive meaning or intelligible content, if this is taken to be constituted by abstract conceptual relations. On the other hand, pragmatic meaning is not intended to point to the use and value of ideas in a way that is superfluous to the question of their import as items of cognition. Pragmatic meaning is intended to bridge the gap between these alternatives, and it is intended by James to replace cognitive meaning as the sense of meaning which is significant enough to be worthy of the philosopher's concern.

4. Moral Value: Good and the Satisfaction of Demand

A COMMON VIEW OF moral value is that actions are in themselves right or wrong, good or bad, desirable or tragic, obligatory, permissible, or forbidden, simply because of the kind of actions they are. The worth of an action is determined by its relation to a preestablished set of moral standards—a set of abstract and unchanging absolute moral principles prescribing what is valuable. Some have held that these values are grounded in an a priori moral law, others that they are recorded in the mind of God, and some have held that they are found in the thoughts of the Absolute; but all who subscribe to this view agree that moral value is independent of the contingencies of particular empirical circumstances and conditions. Believers in an overarching set of moral values are convinced that, notwithstanding the ambiguities and complexities of moral dilemmas as they actually present themselves in our lives, there is a true, unchanging, and solidly grounded answer to each moral question. From their point of view, even if that answer is difficult to discover, the fact that it is there to be found inspires confidence.

In spite of the advantages of a morality of this sort, it has one crucial drawback. Its basis or ground has not always been apparent—even to its believers. God could ground such an absolute morality, and in medieval times metaphysically grounded moral absolutism had more the status of a received doctrine. But in modern

times the philosophical and empirical problems of such
a view have come to predominate over the alternative
of its comforting belief. With the Darwinian revolution,
the notion of an eternal preexistent moral order lost
much of its appeal. For James and others of his time,
Darwinism was the near-final affirmation that scientific
method and empirical relationships could furnish a
model for truth not only in science but in other diverse
fields as well. One cannot help but notice a similarity
between the Darwinian notions of "the struggle for
existence" and the "survival of the fittest," and the
major claim of James's ethics that "the essence of good
is simply to satisfy demand." Darwinism in ethics was to
take its own course, and have its own history. And
James's ethics carries, as expected, his own indelible
stamp. But he is nonetheless allied with those who reject the absolute and a priori in ethics, and instead em-
brace the empirical order as the foundation of moral
value.

In spite of his admiration for the strenuousness of
the commitment engendered by belief in an absolute
moral order, James nevertheless rejects any conception
of morality under which moral value is considered to
be independent of concrete actions, events, feelings,
and judgments. Moral goodness and badness, rightness, wrongness, and obligation, in James's judgment,
are expressed and grounded from within the context
of real moral activities—aims posited, goals achieved,
feelings respected, compromises made, and the like. In
this chapter we shall examine how James constructs an
ethical system on these terms, and consider the meaning, justification, and implications of his position.

There are two major doctrines in James's philosophy
which serve well in understanding his ethical theory.
The first is his theory of meaning, the second his notion of human nature as being essentially goal-directed
and interest-laden. James wrote only one essay on ethical theory—"The Moral Philosopher and the Moral
Life"—and this was published seven years prior to
"Philosophical Conceptions and Practical Results," in

which he first articulates his theory of meaning.[1] Given this chronology, it would be too much to say that James analyzes moral concepts in terms of any developed theory of meaning. Nevertheless, the basic insight that would later become his developed theory of meaning is solidly embodied in this earlier ethical work. As the pragmatic meaning of metaphysical and scientific claims is determined by their concrete and specific consequences in the lives of individuals, James insists on the same standard for the pragmatic meaning of ethical claims. Eschewing principles of morality which are not grounded in concrete and particular fact, his ethical stance follows naturally. His position is an ethical naturalism—he characterizes moral value in exclusively empirical terms.

The second major aspect of James's philosophy which influences his ethical theory is his conception of human nature. As we have seen in Chapter 2, James conceives of human beings as conative, striving, desiring, purposive, idealizing, and goal-oriented in nature, attempting to fulfill their diverse ends as best they can. For James, the pursuit of the fulfillment of these ends is the central activity of a human being—indeed, it may be said, the central meaning of his life. As such, it follows naturally that the fulfillment of goals, ideals, purposes, desires, and the like will be the locus of moral value in James's system.

James devotes himself to two basic philosophical questions in "The Moral Philosopher and the Moral Life." [2] He calls these the "metaphysical question" and the "casuistic question." The metaphysical question is concerned with the *meaning* of the most important ethical terms—"good," "bad," and "obligation"—and with the foundation of moral value. The "casuistic question" pertains to the *measure* of moral value. Whatever qualities turn out to constitute moral goodness, one must still have a criterion for determining how good anything is. The measure of moral value is necessary if we are to know which actions, events, or states of affairs are better than others, and what our actual obligations are. We will consider the metaphysical and casuistic questions in turn.

I

In James's discussion of the "metaphysical question," designed to determine the "meaning" of moral terms, he sets out a hypothetical situation which is intended to prove that the existence of sentient life is necessary for the existence of moral value. In order to show this, James asks the reader to picture a world without sentient life. He asks us to consider whether it would make sense to say of that world that some things in it were better or worse than others.

> Imagine an absolutely material world, containing only physical and chemical facts, and existing from eternity without a God, without even an interested spectator: would there be any sense in saying of that world that one of its states is better than another?[3]

James asks us further to imagine that there are two such worlds; and he holds that we will be unable to find any intrinsic moral difference between them. James's point is that there could be no value independent of any reference to sentient beings. In making a judgment here one must take special care, James warns, to leave one's own preferences out of account. For to call one world better than another on the basis of one's own preferences is once again to have attributed value on the basis of someone's feelings — this time one's own — and this is *contra hypothesi*.

In judging the case fairly, one must imagine a world where no consciousness exists, and hence where no judgments of value are possible. James concludes from this example that the existence of sentient life is necessary for moral value:

> Surely there is no *status* for good and evil to exist in, in a purely insentient world. How can one physical fact, con-

sidered simply as a physical fact, be "better" than another? Betterness is not a physical relation. In its mere material capacity, a thing can no more be good or bad than it can be pleasant or painful.[4]

James then goes on to have us imagine a single person in the otherwise insentient universe he has described. James calls this state of affairs a "moral solitude." With the coming into the world of that person — with his desires, aims, feelings, and judgments — James claims, moral values also come into existence:

> The moment one sentient being, however, is made a part of the universe, there is a chance for goods and evils really to exist. Moral relations now have their *status*, in that being's consciousness. So far as he feels anything to be good, he *makes* it good. It *is* good, for him; and being good for him, is absolutely good, for he is the sole creator of values in that universe, and outside of his opinion things have no moral character at all.[5]

Morality comes to exist, James believes, because moral value consists in the fulfillment of demands of sentient creatures. As James puts it, "the essence of good is simply to satisfy demand." [6]

The notion of the satisfaction of demand is the most central concept in James's ethical theory; yet he is never careful to specify what he means by the term "demand." It has not hitherto been recognized that James seems to use the notion in several senses without considering important any distinctions that might be made among them. One sense he attaches to the notion of "demand" comes into play when he sets out to establish the foundation of moral value. In this context, when James speaks of a demand, frequently he is referring to anything anyone desires, aims for, or cares about. On this sense, a demand is a felt positive interest.[7] Another sense of "demand" used by James depends upon judgment. To demand something in this sense is to judge it to be good.[8] Finally, James relies on a third sense of "demand," one to which he appeals when describing how we are in practice to go about discovering the morally best arrangement among persons whose demands conflict. This third sense of the term reflects more than the others the common use of "demand" in our language. On this conception, a demand is an imperative. To demand is to order or dictate or command that one receive something, or that some state of affairs comes to pass.[9]

Thus James uses the notion of demand in three different senses: demand as interest, demand as judgment, and demand as command. Obviously, these different senses of the term have different implications, and later in this chapter we will consider a significant problem to which these differences give rise. For the purposes of our present discussion, however, we shall simply adopt James's use of the term. In James's consideration of the grounding of moral value—the issue presently before us—he thinks of demand as a felt positive interest and as a judgment of value. The range of demands may be inexhaustible. Demands may be simple desires for immediate bodily pleasures, more long-range aims such as career goals, and even such abstract ideals as justice, honesty, freedom, and the like.

James's position is a thoroughgoing naturalism: moral value is fully constituted by the satisfaction of demand. If a person has a demand for something, no matter what that thing may be, it is good that that demand be satisfied. Nothing outside of demands has any relevance whatever to the moral value of things, for there is nowhere besides conscious life for that value to gain a foothold. And with no possibility of an independent realm of value against which we might test their validity, all demands are necessarily above question. In holding that all demands are valid—"the demand may be for anything under the sun" [10]—James does not fail to recognize that demands inevitably conflict, and that in cases of conflict it will be better to fulfill some demands over others. He does not hold that anything which satisfies any demand is automatically good over-all. Rather, his point is that qua providing the satisfaction of demand, an act, event, or object is good:

> Take any demand, however slight, which any creature, however weak, may make. Ought it not, for its own sole sake, to be satisfied? If not, prove why not. The only possible kind of proof you could adduce would be the exhibition of another creature who should make a demand that ran the other way. The only possible reason there can be why any phenomenon ought to exist is that such a phenomenon actually is desired.[11]

How could something be morally bad if it satisfied someone's demand and if no one objected to it? What would make it morally bad if no one felt it to be so? How could the satisfaction of demand in itself be anything but good?

James has put his case persuasively. If one is asked to explain why a person's demand should not be met in the absence of any countervailing demand, one is put into a curious and difficult position. By hypothesis, we have a demand that interferes with no one. And it seems plausible to hold that the existence of conflicting demands is the only possible reason that can be held against the fulfillment of any demand.

A significant aspect of James's position is that it places full moral authority within the individual himself. If an individual *considers* something to be good, then that *makes* it good. While it may not, once all demands are considered, turn out to be good over-all, still its prima facie goodness is determined by its being demanded. The ground of value is in the individual's demands, and whatever fulfills those demands cannot be immoral. The state of moral solitude, previously described, is the strongest device James has for making the point that the satisfaction of demand is necessarily good. In a world with only one sentient being, James argues, it makes no sense whatever to reject the satisfaction of any demand as immoral, since there exists no other creature from whose standpoint that judgment could be made. In the moral solitude the satisfaction of the thinker's demands is not merely prima facie good. It is unconditionally good. Hence moral value depends entirely upon the demands of the solitary thinker himself.

Although this position is appealing, it becomes problematic when considered from another point of view, even in the context of a moral solitude. Let us imagine an individual living alone in the world, with an abundance of all things he wants or needs. Let us imagine also that instead of choosing to educate his mind in whatever way he can, refine his sensibilities, and strengthen and develop his body, he prefers instead to develop none of his potentialities, in fact to waste them all—learning nothing, doing little, and in short, reducing himself to a near-vegetative state. Granting that the individual himself may think that his life is good, it seems reasonable to hold that in fact it is not good, or at least not as good as several other alternatives open to him. In short, even in a moral solitude, it may not be good that the individual's demands be satisfied.

Or consider the following: first, a world of individuals devoted to resolving their differences by means of physical assault, considering combat to be the only noble way for resolving disputes, and admiring battle, violence, and the affirmation of personal power over others. Second, a world identical to the first except that differences are resolved amicably and peacefully. In both worlds, as we are picturing them, the sentient beings are fulfilling their demands to the maximal possible degree; and the only morally relevant difference between the two worlds lies in the *kinds* of demands they are having satisfied. On James's principle that the satisfaction of demand is ipso facto good, these alternative worlds must be equal in moral value. It seems clear, however, that the second world is morally preferable to the first. But if this is so, then James's principle does not enable us to make the moral choices that seem to us to be most correct.

Some demands are for things that are not good (or

not as good as other alternatives), and it is not good (or at least not optimal) that these demands be satisfied. It is far better that certain immoral or morally non-optimal demands be redirected or eliminated. But if only some demands, and not others, are good, or if some are better than others, there must be a criterion for distinguishing which of them are good and ought to be satisfied, and which are not. But if this is the case, then it is not the fact that something is demanded which makes it good. It is some other quality, independent of its being demanded, which determines its moral worth.

James also argues for the converse of the position we have been examining. He holds not only that satisfying a demand is sufficient for something's being good. He contends also that it is necessary—if something is to be good it must satisfy a demand:

> Nothing can be good or right except so far as some consciousness feels it to be good or thinks it to be right.[12]

> "Good," "bad," and "obligation" . . . .mean no absolute natures, independent of personal support. They are objects of feeling and desire, which have no foothold or anchorage in Being, apart from the existence of actually living minds.[13]

Here we find the metaphysical status of moral value firmly placed in James's theory. He rejects any conception of morality as a priori, or as existing in any way independent of conscious beings. Goodness, badness, rightness, and wrongness are fully grounded in the experiential world. Moral value must be felt in order to exist. Quite simply, in the phrase James borrows from Berkeley, its *"esse* is *percipi."* [14]

James's ethical theory presents an antidote to the more abstract moral absolutisms of some of his contemporaries. Yet in his attempt to establish a concrete grounding for moral value, he has swung rather far in the opposite direction. In attempting fully to explain morality in terms of the mental states of conscious beings, he eliminates as part of his theory any reference to unperceived value. But to leave no room for presently unperceived possibilities for moral betterment is to miss the full significance of the moral enterprise. Let us consider some examples.

There have always been instances of persons who are oppressed—whose freedoms are limited, rights violated, and means of self-expression and self-actualization suppressed by those in power. It is a serious moral evil in situations of this sort that the oppressed persons do not have their demands satisfied. A more serious evil, however, is that these persons may be manipulated into a situation where they do not even have the demands it would be best to have. The point behind current "liberation" movements, for example, is not merely to educate oppressed classes as to how to get what they want more easily. More importantly, it is to show oppressed persons, who have been content with their lives, that such contentment is unjustified. The point in other words is not—as James sees it— that the good is embodied in *existing* demands, but rather that demands ought to be *generated* in order to embody what is good. Given this, some states of affairs could clearly be good, yet not satisfy an existing felt demand.

Education provides another example in which the ideal of changing demands is operative. Whatever else may be involved, one set of goals appropriate to education is the instillment of certain sorts of demands (for example, love of learning and critical thinking), the refinement of others (for example, aesthetic or moral demands), and even the elimination of some (for example, demands for extensive, passive non-intellectual activity).[15] Thus education is built upon the idea of a state of affairs which would be good, although it satisfies no presently felt demand.

My aim in this discussion has been to show that moral value is not identical to the satisfaction of demand, and thus that James's position on the foundation of morality is flawed in significant ways. I should now like to examine one of the ways in which James would reply to this criticism, as it will clarify certain basic assumptions in his theory. Regarding the argument that the satisfaction of some demands is not good—for example, that it is not good for a person to spend his life merely vegetating even though that meets his demands—James would point out that in criticizing this person the critic must necessarily do so in terms of his own moral values. One can evaluate another's demands only by reference to his own. Similarly, against the point that some things, for example self-actualization, are good even if there is no demand for them, James would maintain that one would have no reason to make this claim unless he himself held self-actualization to be valuable—that is to say, had a demand for it, with reference either to himself or to others. James's main point is this: it makes no sense to hold that moral value exists independently of some conscious being's moral evaluation. For to hold that something is morally valuable is no more than to value it from the standpoint of one's own interests and demands.

As we have seen, James uses Berkeley's phrase "*esse* is *percipi*" to describe the status of moral value. The essence of his argument is Berkeleyan as well. In the *Principles*, Berkeley argues against the materiality of physical objects by challenging his reader to imagine the existence of trees, books, etc., with no one there to perceive them. Berkeley contends that this is impossible, for any attempt to imagine unperceived objects necessarily, albeit implicitly, makes reference to a perceiver. To the individual allegedly imagining the existence of unperceived objects, Berkeley responds:

What is all this, I beseech you, more than framing in *your* mind certain ideas which you call books and trees, and at the same time omitting to frame the idea of any one that may perceive them? But do not you yourself perceive or think of them all the while? This therefore is nothing to the purpose: it only shews you have the power of imagin-

ing or forming ideas in your mind; but it does not shew
that you can conceive it possible the objects of your
thought may exist without the mind. To make out this, it is
necessary that *you* conceive them existing unconceived or
unthought of, which is a manifest repugnancy.[16]

Berkeley's most important mistake was to infer from
the fact that we have to think of things in order to posit
their existence independently of our thought, that they
therefore cannot exist unthought of. That we must
think about an unperceived object in order to posit its
existence does not prove that the object itself must
have been thought about in order to exist.

James falls into the same sort of mistake. He takes
the philosophical question, "What is it that constitutes
moral value?," and reduces it to the empirical question,
"What is it that individuals take to be valuable—i.e.,
what is it that they demand?" But it should be clear
that this reduction is unwarranted. One would be quite
correct in the observation—indeed it is tautological—
that *attributions* of moral value can occur only in the
context of some individual making moral evaluations.
But it is not justifiable to infer from this that moral
values themselves cannot exist independently of these
attributions. James makes a great deal of sense in his
notion that morality would be meaningless in the absence of sentient life. But given that sentient life is required for morality, it does not follow that felt demands determine how moral value shall be constituted.
Some things may be better or worse for sentient beings
even though they may fail to recognize them to be so.

We must conclude, then, that James's view, which interprets morality as exclusively and exhaustively
understandable in terms of that which is consciously
appropriated as valuable, is impoverished in significant
ways. Still, the empirical motivation behind James's system seems quite reasonable. James is right in his suspi-
cions of a non-empirical foundation of morality, for it
seems quite clear that, short of any knowledge of a
transexperiential ground of value, one should aim for

an ethical theory which is empirically based. Indeed, most would agree that, even though one cannot deduce normative propositions from factual ones, in formulating ethical principles we must still make the most extensive possible use of any factual knowledge we may have about human beings and their condition. But, given this commitment to an empirical approach, we may still accept that there are considerations outside of James's scheme of felt valuations which are relevant and important. Thus, the conclusions about human nature to be found in the social and certain of the natural sciences—to the extent that they are sound—cannot meaningfully be ignored if one is to formulate a viable ethical system. We know enough about human nature to say reasonably that some sorts of things are valuable, or at least more valuable than others. The fact that human beings have, for example, certain genetic predispositions, certain characteristic personality patterns, certain individual talents and unique potentialities, and a rather distinct set of biological and emotional conditions under which they function optimally (in some reasonably uncontroversial sense of that term) ought to make a difference to our moral system—even if these characteristics do not always find expression in the satisfaction of felt demands.

These points being made, let us now turn to another aspect of James's ethical philosophy—one which appears to be entirely different from the view we have been considering thus far. We have just seen that a central element in James's ethical theory as it appears in "The Moral Philosopher" is his view that the best world would be one in which any demand whatsoever was satisfied as soon as it was made. One aspect of this position which might make us loathe to accept it is that it appears to sanction self-indulgence. If the immediate satisfaction of demand were the highest good, there would be no meaning to the idea of forsaking the fulfillment of some demands for the sake of those that were better or higher. Thus there would appear to be no room on this view of morality for moral sacrifice

and commitment, heroism and moral strenuousness.
Yet James elsewhere in his writings is an enthusiastic
champion of just such moral rigorousness. He argues
explicitly against the moral lassitude and indifference
he believes inevitably accompany the more extreme
forms of subjectivism. He rejects the idea that the
higher ideals are not worth fighting for, and he would
consider someone morally blind who thought ethical
notions to be empty of objective and compelling status
and pertinence.[17] Indeed, in many of James's works we
find a view that appears to be in direct conflict with the
main points of the satisfaction of demand theory. In
"The Dilemma of Determinism," for example, James
claims that the best state from a moral point of view is
not the satisfaction of demand or the achievement of
good, but rather the *attempt* to achieve it: "Not the absence of vice, but vice there, and virtue holding her by
the throat, seems the ideal human state." [18] In the
Principles of Psychology James very powerfully describes
the way in which he thinks human beings aim toward
their own progressive moral development.[19] Noteworthy in this discussion is the fact that James finds the
process—the strenuous attempt to achieve their own
better selves—essential from the moral point of view.
In "The Moral Equivalent of War," again James emphasizes not ideals or demands *as fulfilled* as being
worthwhile, but rather the moral value of the process
of energetic and vigorous attempts to fulfill them.[20]

How can the apparent conflict between James's satisfaction of demand theory in "The Moral Philosopher"
and his emphasis on moral strenuousness elsewhere be
reconciled? One way might be by making a distinction
between James's strictly theoretical claims in "The
Moral Philosopher" and the more practical moral proposals in his other works. It may be that while James
holds to the theoretical point that "the best simply
imaginary world would be one in which *every* demand
was gratified as soon as made,"[21] he nevertheless realizes that this ideal world is not the one in which we
live. James recognizes the existence of evil in the

world,[22] and he also accepts the fact that as a practical matter it is impossible to satisfy all demands at all times.[23] Thus, his view might be that while ideally the immediate satisfaction of demand is best, on the practical level the extent to which our demands are in fact satisfied will depend upon the degree of our energy and commitment devoted to fulfilling them. Thus, from a practical point of view, the moral injunction would be to aim strenuously at as much good as possible. This interpretation of James's view is strengthened by the fact that he holds that we will never reach the morally ideal state of affairs "until the last man has had his say." [24] He contends that "our moral horizon moves with us as we move," [25] and hence that our situation will always be one in which moral improvement, and hence strenuousness, is called for.

While I suggest this interpretation because it goes a long way toward integrating James's seemingly diverse views, nevertheless it may not be viable. For a closer look at James shows that he values moral strenuousness not merely as a means of overcoming obstacles which in a perfect world would not be there, but also as a quality which is itself intrinsically valuable. Thus in his article "Is Life Worth Living?," James makes the following observation:

> It is, indeed, a remarkable fact that sufferings and hardships do not, as a rule, abate the love of life; they seem, on the contrary, usually to give it a keener zest. The sovereign source of melancholy is repletion. Need and struggle are what excite and inspire us; our hour of triumph is what brings the void.[26]

James applies his observation to a concrete case in his essay "What Makes a Life Significant?" Here he tells of his visit several years before to a utopian community at Chautauqua Lake, in which the ideals of civilization have been successfully fulfilled. He reports that there is health, security, ample outlet for intellectual, physical, aesthetic, and religious expression. There is culture, lawfulness, and equality. There is no poverty or suffer-

ing. But James rejects this community as morally fatu-
ous precisely because it is one in which demands are
immediately satisfied.

> But what our human emotions seem to require is the sight
> of the struggle going on. The moment the fruits are being
> merely eaten, things become ignoble. Sweat and effort,
> human nature strained to its uttermost and on the rack,
> yet getting through alive, and then turning its back on its
> success to pursue another more rare and arduous still—
> this is the sort of thing the presence of which inspires
> us. . . . [27]

But if moral strenuousness is itself a desideratum for
James, how can this fact be reconciled with his theory
of the satisfaction of demand? The answer, I suggest,
lies in a more complex understanding of the kinds of
demands persons have. Along with our demands for
external ends, such as food, companionship, or justice,
we may also have self-regarding demands concerning
the extent and value of our own potencies. Thus James
contends that we demand that our goals be realized not
by the objects of our desire merely being given to us,
but rather as the result of our own efforts. We demand
that we have an active and even heroic part to play in
the achievement of good results.[28] In this way the
possibility of moral strenuousness on James's view is
reconciled with the principles of his ethical theory.

While this proposal shows that there is no contradic-
tion in James's view, there is still a related point which
must be addressed. Even if the ideal of strenuousness is
not inconsistent with the theory of the satisfaction of
demand, James himself finds that it appears to be
gratuitous. He observes that on his own empiricist,
naturalistic ethical theory there seems little reason for
taking the strenuous stance, in spite of the fact that we
all have inclinations toward it. If morality were
grounded merely on the demands of finite creatures,
James claims, there would be little point in making
great sacrifices. For the sacrifices would be on behalf of
persons who are in no particular measure more

worthy—or at least no more loved—than ourselves.[29] It is for this reason that James finds it appropriate to posit the existence of God as a practical postulate. Only belief in God, James thinks, can provide persons with sufficient external justification for acting according to their natural tendencies toward moral strenuousness. One might well wonder whether James is correct in his belief that human beings fail to see the welfare of other persons as maximally compelling from the moral point of view, or that they require a God to motivate their strongest moral effort. The existence of many thoroughly dedicated humanists would seem to count against this claim. Nevertheless, from James's point of view, while a moral system is possible without a God, it would not be one that is optimally satisfying. Only a theologically based morality will be as powerful as we want it to be:

> Even if there were no metaphysical or traditional grounds for believing in a God, men would postulate one simply as a pretext for living hard, and getting out of the game of existence its keenest possibilities of zest.[30]

James finds it important to make the psychological point that belief in God generates moral strenuousness, but he also wants to go further than this. He goes on to draw some provisional conclusions about God's actual existence in terms of the role His existence plays in the constitution of morality. In the final section of "The Moral Philosopher" James expresses his belief that the conflicting and ephemeral felt demands of finite subjects—each having no greater authority than any other—can never provide an adequate basis for an ideally and conclusively objective system of values. He holds that such an ethical system—in his terms a "systematically unified moral truth"[31]—can exist only if there exists a God, a divine demander by whose fiat the relative value of goods would be constituted. It is only under God's infinite viewpoint that the ideal limit of a stable and fully objective moral system would obtain.[32] The postulate of God, then, would lend legitimacy and authority to one particular system of demands over others—render it final, correct, and ultimate.

While James poses this view, he is nevertheless sensitive enough to the limitations set by his own empiricism to realize that the postulate of God's existence can be used by us only as the basis for projecting a moral ideal and not as a substantive grounding of any functioning ethical system. For James realizes that we lack conclusive evidence that there exists such a divine consciousness, and we lack as well conclusive evidence for what His hierarchy of demands would be.[33] Life in a world without a God is indeed a "genuinely ethical symphony," [34] James maintains, and in solving our concrete moral problems, we must fall back on an exclusively empirical assessment of the diverse demands of individuals, and the means by which they can best be satisfied. This James deals with under the second philosophical question he sets for himself in "The Moral Philosopher"—the casuistic question—to which we shall now turn.

II

We have now seen how James establishes a standard of value—"the essence of good is simply to satisfy demand." But without a method of application, such a standard would have no point. Given that the essence of good is the satisfaction of demand, how do we decide in actual life situations which things are good, which things are bad, and which things are better than others? How can the principle of the satisfaction of demand be applied in solving concrete moral problems? James's aim in his discussion of "the casuistic question" is to set out guidelines for applying this principle, so that in any particular situation we may have a way of determining the relative values of the alternative choices before us.

James takes as his starting point his judgment that "all demands as such are *prima facie* respectable," [35] and hence that the morally best situation would be one in which *"every* demand was gratified as soon as made." [36] An ideal world would include the possibility of "spending our money, yet growing rich; taking our holiday, yet getting ahead with our work; shooting and fishing, yet doing no hurt to the beasts; gaining no end of experience, yet keeping our youthful freshness of heart." [37] The actual world, however, renders this solution inapplicable, since inevitably some of the individual's demands will conflict with other of his demands, leaving it impossible for them all to be fulfilled at once. Indeed, along with conflict of demands within an individual, there are conflicts among the demands of one individual and those of others. Jones and Smith cannot simultaneously be president of the same corporation, be class valedictorian, or each marry the same person. Given these unavoidable conflicts among demands, and given the fact that all demands, qua demands, are equal in value, how are we to decide which demands are to take precedence over others? If there is no characteristic in the nature of the demands themselves that permits us to call one better than another, then how can relative value be determined?

James's answer in "The Moral Philosopher" is that since, in the ideal situation, all demands would be satisfied as soon as they were made, and that since the ideal state of affairs is not possible, the best possible world is one in which the ideal is most nearly approached. This means that the best state of affairs is the one that results in the "richer universe," in the most *inclusive* satisfaction of demand:

Since everything which is demanded is by that fact a good, must not the guiding principle for ethical philosophy . . . be simply to satisfy at all times *as many demands as we can?* That act must be the best act, accordingly, which makes for the *best whole*, in the sense of awakening the least sum of dissatisfactions. In the casuistic scale, therefore, those ideals must be written highest which *prevail at the least cost*, or by whose realization the least possible number of other ideals are destroyed. Since victory and defeat there must be, the victory to be philosophically prayed for is that of the more inclusive side—of the side which even in the hour of triumph will to some degree do justice to the ideals in which the vanquished party's interests lay.[38]

Most interesting about James's proposal here is the fact that while the satisfaction of demand is taken as the only criterion of moral value, nevertheless he does not utilize a merely quantitative test of what is right. Rather, he recognizes that there is an internal complexity to demands, and that they may be satisfied in different respects or dimensions, and in different degrees. In any particular situation of moral choice, the key to determining the best state of affairs lies in the idea of the inclusivity of the satisfaction of demand, and this involves reconciling and harmonizing as many demands as possible. Given that some demands inevitably will be more fully satisfied than others, the optimal state of affairs will embody the most just distribution of satisfactions. Specifically, the morally best arrangement will be that compromise which results in the smallest possible number of demands being totally unsatisfied, in the context of the greatest number of demands being satisfied—each to the greatest possible extent and in the greatest number of respects. There is no way in which the fulfillment of these conditions can be measured in strictly quantitative terms. In making moral decisions one must aim rather for a judgment— in some ways qualitative—as to the correct balance between the extent to which and the dimensions in which each of these interdependent conditions is fulfilled.[39]

James's best-known application of the principle of the inclusive satisfaction of demand is found in his essay "The Moral Equivalent of War." In this essay, James's aim is to find a way to satisfy in the most inclusive possible way the rival demands on the one hand for peace, and on the other hand for the establishment and perpetuation of the martial qualities of hardihood and discipline, honor, disinterestedness, and a willingness to make sacrifices. The reconciliation James advocates is the establishment of an army of sorts, but one that does not war against human beings. James suggests that the best way to find expression for the preferred "martial virtues" is by conscription of the whole youthful population for the performance of physical labor in the "warfare against nature." He proposes that the young people be required to work hard at manual labor for the sake of civic pride, and for the benefit of the society as a whole. James points out as an additional advantage of this plan that it will eliminate the unjust condition of society in which only some are forced to do manual labor, while the non-strenuous life of others is parasitic upon them. He enumerates other beneficial consequences of the arrangement as well. In "The Moral Equivalent of War" James is concerned to show the advantages of his proposal from as many different aspects as possible. As such, the essay provides a good illustration of the diverse kinds of considerations that come into play in determining which social arrangement results in the richest, most inclusive satisfaction of demands.

It should be clear that there is no way to say in advance how any reconciliation of demands will turn out best. The problem of how to satisfy demands most inclusively is an empirical and experimental one, requiring in each situation an appreciation of what is at stake from all sides, and sensitivity in balancing all opposing claims. Every situation of moral choice is constituted by a unique configuration of demands, conflicts, and concrete possibilities of satisfaction—satisfaction of varying degrees and varying respects. As is to be expected, then, the solutions to moral problems are not deducible from abstract rules. Such rules may provide some help, James claims, "but they help the less in proportion as our intuitions are more piercing, and our vocation is the stronger for the moral life." [40]

In James's consideration of applied moral judgments, it is surprising to note that his discussion of the reconciliation of demands focuses only on issues of major social decision-making, leaving us perplexed as to guidelines for solving individual moral conflicts.[41] In the context of social policy-making—for example, in the context of decisions about the value of the marriage institution, the free-enterprise system, or social-welfare programs—James sees moral judgments as having the character of hypotheses that exist as embodied in social institutions. And this is the form in which they are tested for their acceptability. As we have seen, the more inclusively a social arrangement satisfies demands, the more acceptable it will be.

But what is the test for the satisfaction of demands? How does one determine how inclusively satisfying a particular social arrangement is? The test, as James sees it, is quite simply its survival. A social scheme is acceptable to the extent that it survives. And it survives to the extent that it fails to generate complaints. James holds that the "cries of the wounded" will bring to light the inadequacy of social systems which fail to satisfy demands with sufficient inclusivity.[42] Any social arrangement that is not sufficiently inclusive in its satisfaction of demand, James contends, will "be overthrown by any newly discovered order which will hush up the complaints that [the old arrangement] give[s] rise to, without producing others louder still." [43] Social experiments are "to be judged, not a priori, but by actually finding, after the fact of their making, how much more outcry or how much appeasement comes about." [44]

The essence of good is the satisfaction of demand. If demands are not satisfied, the persons who are dissatisfied will complain; old systems will be overthrown, James believes, and new and better ones will replace them. Under this rigorous test of human rejection and complaint, the biases of particular interest groups or individuals will be overcome, and we will move progressively closer to the ideal of the fully objective ethical system, under which all demands are most inclusively satisfied. Thus James's belief in the inevitability of moral progress relates integrally to the rest of his ethical philosophy.

Looking at James's response to the casuistic question as a whole, we find that there are a number of aspects of his view which are open to criticism. The most important issue in this regard concerns the fact that James relies almost exclusively on the imperative sense of the term "demand" in providing a criterion for measuring moral value. To "demand" in this sense, it will be remembered, means to dictate, order, or command that one receive something, or that some state of affairs come to pass. We distinguished this sense of "demand" from two other senses James attaches to the term—first, where a demand is a felt positive interest; and second, where to have a demand for something is to judge it to be good; and we saw that James does not distinguish between these. It should be noticed however, that it is altogether common for a thing to be demanded in the sense of being judged to be good, or in the sense of being the object of a felt positive interest, without its being demanded in the imperative sense at all. Of particular interest to us here is the separability of demand as interest, and demand as command. There is an important difference between *having* a demand (having a felt positive interest in something), and *making* a demand (dictating, ordering, or commanding). It is certainly morally just, indeed indispensable, to include in calculations of moral value respect for the demands (that is to say, interests) *had* by all members of society. This would include consideration for the demands had by infants, persons with severe physical or mental debilities, and probably even animals. Yet these individuals are frequently unable to *make* demands in the sense we have described. Moreover, though those persons who are capable of making demands may not always choose to do so, it is clearly wrong to discriminate against them on that account. An individual's moral rights are not the sorts of things for which he must make a demand in order to have. Indeed, it is only if an individual has a prior and independent moral right to whatever it is he is demanding, that he is justified in making that demand at all. It must be concluded, then, that James goes too far in relying so heavily on the imperative sense of demand in his analysis of the measurement of moral value.

Moving to a related point, it seems unlikely that James's faith in moral progress can be justified. His view here appears to be that if those members of society who are being unjustly treated would only make their demands known with sufficient clarity, then social arrangements will be changed to accommodate them. A glimpse of social history, however, shows that there is little reason to expect this to be true. The powerless may complain exceedingly and in great numbers, but this in itself often has been shown to provide little motive for social betterment on behalf of those in control. Perhaps James does not actually intend social progress to rely on mere public outcry, but means rather to suggest that if sufficient numbers of persons are frustrated, they will develop the power to insure that their demands be satisfied. For as the history of political activism has shown, it is primarily when the demands of oppressed persons become backed by force that social change may be expected. Even if this proposal were true, however, a problem would remain. While it is quite true that, from a practical point of view, social arrangements which satisfy many persons are likely to be better than those which fail to do so, still from a theoretical perspective there is no guarantee that such arrangements are morally right. For as we have argued, the fact that demands are satisfied does not by itself determine ethical value.

5. Rationality and the Will to Believe

A CHARACTERISTIC THEME in James's philosophy is the view that non-rational factors such as emotional preference and spiritual need may function as the basis for certain individual beliefs. From a psychological point of view, as opposed to classical conceptions of human nature, James makes much of the fact that human beings are not primarily rational. As we have seen in Chapter 2, James sees the most fundamental aspect of the human organism to be its conative character: the fact of striving, desiring, and constructing ends is paramount in human life, and the fulfillment of purposes and interests is stronger than any merely intellectual rules or principles. James does not rest content with this psychological doctrine, but goes on to draw from it philosophical implications of great magnitude. If the conative aspects of life are stronger than the intellectual, then purely intellectual justifications of belief which take no account of human needs, goals, and desires cannot be appropriate. Not only do human aims *motivate* the acceptance of some beliefs over others, on James's view in many cases they also *justify* them. James calls his defense of non-rational belief a defense of "faith," or alternatively, a justification of believing "on passional grounds." When in several of his works James goes to specify precisely what he means by holding a belief on "faith" or on "passional grounds" his definitions are not always fully compatible. Still they all embody the same basic idea: a person holds a belief on faith when he commits himself to that belief because it satisfies certain of his emotional, spiritual, or other personal desires or goals, even though in terms of the evidence for the belief it is insufficiently justified.[1] While an analysis of the meaning and justification of believing on faith for some purposes would include reference to characteristic feelings, intentions, attitudes, and dispositions of the believer, this is not to the point here. The major philosophical interest of James's justification of faith is centered on the idea that to believe on faith is to hold a belief in advance of adequate evidence, and it is this idea to which we shall devote our attention. Thus I shall use the terms "faith," "belief on faith," and "belief on passional grounds" to indicate that the belief in question does not have adequate evidential support.

Few would disagree with James's psychological point that in fact people do hold beliefs on non-rational grounds. But many have disagreed that any philosophical conclusions can be drawn from this. They reject James's view that spiritual or emotional considerations provide any sort of justification for believing whatsoever. Philosophers have typically held that rational grounds alone are appropriate for justifying beliefs. Not unexpectedly, then, when James first presented his views they fell upon the ears of many hostile critics, and controversy over his position continues into the present day. His view often has been thought to be philosophically disreputable for its supposed irrationalism. In arguing that beliefs may be legitimately held in advance of adequate evidence, James is thought to be encouraging wishful thinking and to be violating common standards of intellectual reasonableness. For if a person may justifiably believe whatever he likes without sufficient evidential support, the critics contend, then on James's view there would be no claim that was too irrational or too frivolous to be legitimately held. Thus, according to his critics, James's proposals sanction, indeed idealize, injudiciousness and prejudice. The tenor of their criticism is that on

James's scheme, anything anyone chose to believe for whatever misplaced reason, or even for no reason at all, would be justified, and the upshot of James's proposal would be to render meaningless all canons of intellectual integrity.

This of course has the appearance of a devastating criticism, and if it were true, one would have to reject James's position as philosophically disreputable. While I hope to show that this criticism is not correct, still James must bear some measure of the responsibility for being interpreted in this way. His justification of faith is elaborate, and while he manages to mention all the points necessary to make his case, his proposals are scattered, and several of his arguments are obscure and unclarified. My aim here is to render precise James's proofs and to develop previously unnoticed arguments. This will help resolve the controversy, since to this day both critics and defenders have missed important points in James's argument. We will then be able to assess in detail the charge of irrationalism made against him.

I

James's arguments justifying faith have their meaning bound closely to the contexts in which they were presented, and I should like to make several observations about this before moving to the arguments themselves. Of James's essays, the most important one for justifying faith is "The Will to Believe." This essay was first delivered as an address to the Philosophical Clubs of Yale and Brown universities. James's audience was an academic one, and he sees his listeners—both at this lecture and generally—as being uncritically imbued with a narrow positivistic scientific spirit. He sees them as being uncritically committed to the views, first, that scientific grounds for belief are the *only* rational grounds for belief; and second, that according to scientific standards, a belief is justified only if it is held on the basis of adequate evidence.[2] James considers both these contentions to be incorrect. Moreover, he considers them intellectually and practically stifling, both individually and for the race as a whole. He believes that exclusive reliance on such a model of justification considerably limits the range of human possibilities in the areas of both thought and action.[3] While the bogey of some is superstition, as James puts it, his own "bogey is desiccation" [4]—that desiccation which derives from being overscrupulous regarding the evidence for one's beliefs, and which results in an intellectual and practical timorousness. Against the allegations of his critics, James claims that his aim is not to encourage intellectual laxity or superstitiousness. Indeed, he asserts that if he were addressing a typical non-academic audience the justification of faith he has given would be inappropriate. He reports that his goal is rather to combat in his audiences, composed of students and academics, the "paralysis of their native capacity for faith" which he considers to be their own form of intellectual limitation.[5] His attempt is to encourage, energize, and show to be legitimate—so long as it is not abused—that capacity of passional belief which, on his account, is the precondition of any meaningful intellectual or practical activity. The challenge for James, of course, is to set out criteria for the acceptable—that is to say, reasonable—scope of believing on passional grounds. He is fully cognizant of this, and his intention is not to argue for the justification of faith simpliciter, but only for its justifiability under certain conditions.

In arguing for his position James is rejecting a traditional and longstanding position in the history of philosophy. Philosophers have frequently identified being justified in holding a belief with having adequate evidence for that belief.[6] Locke, Descartes, and more recently H. H. Price, Bertrand Russell, and A. D. Woozley, to name a few, are among those who have accepted this identification, not to mention James's chief opponent—W. K. Clifford.[7] But if these philosophers are right—if a belief is justified only if the believer has adequate evidence for it—then it would seem to be a reasonable rule that the individual ought to hold that belief only on the condition that he has adequate evidence for it.[8] Alternatively, if one holds that an individual's conviction may be subject to degree, then the rule would be that an individual ought to believe a proposition only to the extent that he has adequate evidence for it. Thus we find expressions of this rule in Bertrand Russell:

> We ought to give to every proposition which we consider as nearly as possible that degree of credence which is warranted by the probability it acquires from the evidence known to us.[9]

and put negatively, in W. K. Clifford:

> It is wrong always, everywhere, and for anyone, to believe anything upon insufficient evidence.[10]

I shall call this rule for belief—that one ought to believe only if (or to the extent that) one has adequate evidence—the "evidentialist rule," and I shall use the name "evidentialist" for a philosopher who adheres to it. The evidentialist's point is more importantly negative than positive, with the main point being that one ought not believe what one cannot rationally support. Simply put, if you do not have adequate evidence for a proposition, then you have no right to believe it.

James rejects the evidentialist rule and defends the right to believe on faith. But there has been little agreement among scholars as to the meaning of his claims and arguments, and there has been insufficient understanding of the conditions under which James considers faith to be justified. James's critics tend to construe his thesis too broadly. They are prone to see him as arguing that faith is justified if a believer meets the minimal requirement of having some real concern or interest in an issue—whenever the option before the subject is a "live" one, in James's terminology.[11] James's defenders, on the other hand, tend to go too far the other way and read him too narrowly. They tend to see James as justifying faith only in those few situations in which the believer is faced with what he calls an "intellectually undecidable genuine option." [12] But James's arguments for faith, though not always readily discernible, are more complex, and more interesting, than either of these interpretations allow. In fact, as I shall show, James sets out *three* different kinds of cases in which belief held in advance of adequate evidence is justified. Moreover, these three cases embody *two* quite different principles for justifying belief.

James's first principle of justification appeals to the consequences—specifically the moral and prudential consequences—which follow from the fact that the individual holds the belief he does. James tries to show that there are situations in which belief held in advance of adequate evidence is justified on the basis of the beneficial effects of believing. He has in mind two different sorts of cases which support his point. The first is the well-known case of the intellectually undecidable genuine option; the second, to be discussed later, is the situation in which faith in a fact is a necessary condition of the existence of that fact.

Looking at the case of the intellectually undecidable genuine option, we find that the subject's being justified in holding his belief in advance of adequate evidence stems from the nature of the option itself. James specifies that by a "genuine option" he means a choice between alternative beliefs which is "live," "forced," and "momentous." [13] An option is "live," in James's terminology, if the alternatives that constitute it each appeal to the subject as a real possibility for belief. The individual finds the alternative propositions interesting and worthy of taking a stand upon. When James calls an option "forced," he means that the individual must choose one of the proposed alternatives. The nature of the forced option, as James conceives it, is seen most clearly when the choice is specified in the simplest possible way—in terms of the subject either accepting or not accepting a single proposition which is a candidate for belief. James specifies that when confronted with a forced option it is impossible for the individual to take a sceptical stance. It is worth noting that James does not mean to claim here that in the case of a forced option one cannot, either as a matter of logic or as a matter of fact, refrain from believing both the proposed proposition and its negation. He means rather that from a *pragmatic* point of view scepticism is identical to disbelief. In the case of a forced option, whatever advantages are to be gained by affirming the proposition at hand are lost if one doubts or denies it. Finally, James describes a "momentous" option as one in which the opportunity is unique, the stake significant, and the decision irreversible. As such, a momentous option is one of great importance in an individual's life—one where much hinges on making the correct choice. James's justification of faith in the case of the intellectually undecidable genuine option relies not only on the fact that the option before the individual is a genuine one, but equally importantly on the fact that it is intellectually undecidable. An option is intellectually undecidable if, at the time the choice must be made, there is no adequate evidence upon the basis of which the individual may believe either of the proposed alternatives.

Now let us envision an individual faced with an intellectually undecidable genuine option: he is confronted with an issue of vital importance, his opportunity is unique and his decision irreversible, on pragmatic grounds he cannot remain sceptical, and yet any non-sceptical stance is evidentially unjustified. In perhaps the most famous passage in "The Will to Believe," James holds that belief under these conditions is not only justified, but even necessary:

> *Our passional nature not only lawfully may, but must, decide an option between propositions, whenever it is a genuine option that cannot by its nature be decided on intellectual grounds. . . .* [14]

In these circumstances the individual "lawfully may" hold a belief on passional grounds—he is justified in believing in advance of adequate evidence—because of the consequences that follow from his doing so. Regarding religious belief, for example, a paradigm case for James of an intellectually undecidable genuine option, James makes it clear that the justification for believing on faith relies on the belief's prudential and moral consequences. Prudentially, if the religious hypothesis is true, James claims, it is to my advantage to believe in God; for if I do not believe, I "forfeit my sole chance in life of getting upon the winning side." [15] If the religious hypothesis is true, James contends, my belief is morally justified as well; for included in the religious hypothesis is the proposition that when I believe in God I am "doing the universe the deepest service [I] can." [16]

To think in this way of the religious hypothesis as being a genuine option is to accept James's theological assumptions, and these may seem dubious to many. That there is an afterlife, that its rewards are restricted to those who have religious faith, that religious belief in some way does service to the universe: none of these propositions could stand as acceptable without a great deal of argument. Still, the particular characteristics of James's example should not be seen to intrude on his general point. There are options that are intellectually undecidable and genuine in his sense, and numerous other examples are possible. Imagine, for instance, a situation where a man suspects that his wife has been unfaithful, but the wife denies it, and there is no way for the man reliably to determine the facts of the case. Let us suppose further that if the man believes that his wife has been unfaithful, or even if he remains undecided, conditions are such that the distrust and suspicion engendered would irreversibly destroy the continuation of the marriage in any significant sense. It is only if the man believes in his wife's trustworthiness that the marriage can be meaningfully preserved.[17] Here we have a clear case of an intellectually undecidable genuine option. It would be reasonable in such a situation—of forced and significant choice which nevertheless cannot be evidentially justified—for the man to believe (at least provisionally) in the wife's fidelity for the sake of the benefits to be gained by such a belief. Indeed, opting for the other alternative in such a situation would be destructive and, assuming that the continuation of the marriage is desired, irrational.

Or consider another example: An individual works for a pharmaceutical company and has considerable influence upon the company's decision regarding the experimental testing on humans of a certain drug that may well have ineradicably harmful consequences, though its effects have not been adequately established. The group is about to decide to test the drug, and the individual is forced to take a stand. He may well be able to prevent the experimentation if he chooses against it. The option is live—it is important to him which decision is made. The choice is momentous—the opportunity is unique, the stakes are high, and the decision irreversible. The option is forced, since a vote to abstain is tantamount to not preventing the morally questionable experimentation. Finally, the option is intellectually undecidable, since the effects of the drug are not clear at the time the individual's decision must be made. Given the situation as specified, it would certainly seem most reasonable to make a pre-evidential decision in this situation, on the basis of purely moral considerations.

Many more examples could be adduced, but I think James's point is clear. In the case of an intellectually undecidable genuine option the individual is faced with a practical decision that must be made. It is a decision that can be made only on practical grounds—that is to say, only by considering the moral, prudential, or other practical consequences of one's choice. Moreover, those consequences are of enormous importance. It would be clearly irrational for the individual in this situation to wait for evidence that is simply not available.

James's analysis of the intellectually undecidable genuine option is worthy of the considerable discussion it has received, but it is not all there is to his justification of faith. Under this first same principle—

according to which beliefs are justified by their consequences—there is another case, one which has not
received adequate attention. The important fact about
it is that it is logically independent of the genuine option situation. This is the case in which belief in a
proposition is a necessary condition of that proposition's being true. There are occasions, James argues,
where the existence of a certain state of affairs is con-
tingent on the subject's first believing that it obtains.
There are situations, involving interpersonal relations
and the fulfillment of personal goals, where believing
that a given proposition is true is necessary to provide
one with the motivation for performing certain actions;
and the performance of these actions, in turn, is a
necessary condition of that proposition's being true.
Thus in situations of this sort the existence of a fact is
dependent on faith. Accordingly, I shall call this situation one in which "faith is necessary for the fact." In
the following passage James clarifies this point and
spells out its epistemological import:

> But in every fact into which there enters an element of
> personal contribution on my part, as soon as this personal
> contribution demands a certain degree of subjective en-
> ergy which, in its turn, calls for a certain amount of faith
> in the result—so that, after all, the future fact is con-
> ditioned by my present faith in it—how trebly asinine
> would it be for me to deny myself the use of the subjective
> method, the method of belief based on desire![18]

James's essays in *The Will to Believe* are rich with
examples of the principle that faith is necessary for the
fact. For instance, he points to collections of individuals
which require cooperative interaction, such as an ath-
letic team, an army, and a government, and observes
that these and other social organisms proceed on the
basis of the faith on the part of each of its members
that the other members will perform their expected
roles.[19] To consider other cases, James points to the
fact that a person's worldly success may well depend
upon his faith in that success—that taking risks and

acting in advance on the faith that one will succeed often provide the best context and motive for achieving that success.[20] In an extensive discussion he argues that even such fundamental issues as whether life is worth living may be determined by each individual's faith that it is. Believing that life is worth living may lead the individual to overcome that which is evil or problematic in his life and to fulfill what is best in himself. As such the belief that life is worth living may verify itself.[21]

There can be little doubt that James has an important insight in his observation that belief held in advance of adequate evidence may be justified on prudential grounds. While there must be appropriate qualifications made regarding the limits of prudential justification, as we shall see below, we may nevertheless conclude at this point that there are cases where the benefits of belief do play an important justificatory role. In developing his case, James argues also that there are instances where belief in advance of adequate evidence is justified on moral grounds. He contends that in circumstances where immediate action is required in order to prevent morally undesirable consequences, and where such action must be grounded in the appropriate belief, then withholding belief because one's evidence is inadequate is immoral. Thus, for example, if one must act at once to save a drowning person or to stop a murder, then it would be immoral not to perform those actions simply because of epistemic uncertainties about the facts of the case.[22] If holding a specific belief is required in order to perform the appropriate action, then holding that belief is justified.

To reiterate our analysis thus far, we have found that James considers it reasonable to believe in advance of adequate evidence when an individual is either (1) confronted with an intellectually undecidable genuine option; or (2) when he is faced with a situation in which faith in a fact is necessary for the existence of that fact.[23] In both of these cases, the belief in question is justified because of its prudential or moral benefits, *in-*

dependently of any appeal to adequate evidence. It is justified solely on the basis of the practical consequences of belief.

At this point quite a serious objection to James's view may be brought forth. It may be held that James fails in his justification of belief by consequences. For when examined closely, in both the case of the genuine option, as well as in the case where faith is necessary for the fact, James appears to be providing a justification not of belief, but rather of action. Looking first at the genuine option situation, one may hold that James's point is vitiated by a central confusion. Besides the case of religious belief, all of James's other cases which could count as genuine options are options not to believe, but to act in certain ways.[24] Even in the case of the religious option, James contends that religious belief is meaningless unless it leads to actions different from those engendered by belief in a non-religious hypothesis, and it appears to be the actions that truly make the difference in James's eyes.[25] It would seem, then, that James's interest lies in options to act. But if this is the case, then in what sense can he be said to have fulfilled his intention of providing a justification of belief?

The same problem occurs in the situations where faith is necessary for the fact. As several of James's critics have pointed out, if the individual's belief is to be justified by the consequences of the actions to which that belief leads, then one need only act *as though* he believed a given proposition to be true, and the same results will follow as from actual belief.[26]

In response to this objection, it should be recognized that James holds that there is a close, if not a necessary connection between belief and action. We have seen in Chapter 2 that James holds either that an individual's thinking is invariably accompanied by action, or at least that thinking generates in the individual a disposition to act in certain ways. Since believing is a kind of thinking, for James the reference to action is essential in any discussion of belief.[27] It should be clear, then, that

James would have rejected as faulty any criticism which was based on the separability of actions and beliefs. We have already seen, however, that there are serious difficulties with James's attempt to tie thought so closely to action, and so we must conclude that this criticism is quite appropriate.

It is therefore important to note at this point that James can make his case even without assuming an invariable link between belief and action. First, it is quite possible for there to be situations in which options to believe, independent of action, do meet the criteria for the intellectually undecidable genuine option situation. In the case above of the man's belief in his wife's faithfulness, the consequences that justify belief need not stem from actions, but may derive exclusively from the beliefs themselves, along with the feelings and emotional commitments that follow upon them. Second, in the cases of options to act, it may be granted that, in abstraction, James's critics are quite correct in drawing the conceptual distinction between believing a proposition and merely acting as though one believed it. Indeed, there are certainly many situations in an individual's life for which this distinction is appropriate.

Nevertheless, it would be psychologically insensitive to insist that such a distinction is always applicable in the affairs of actual life. Consider, for example, James's case of a person, climbing a mountain, who must make a difficult leap across a chasm to save his life. James has us imagine that without the confidence that he can succeed, the person will surely perish.[28] To make the logical point here that in order to succeed, the man need only act *as though* he believed he can make the leap, is to miss entirely the essence of the situation in which he finds himself. The man may well be unable to act as though he can successfully make the leap unless he actually believes that he can. Similarly, the energy required to complete a long-term project that was arduous or painful in many instances would not be forthcoming unless one felt reasonably sure of success. Some actions require the kind of courage or energy which, as a matter of fact, simply will not be available without the subjective support of actual commitment.

Let us now examine the second principle on the basis of which James justifies passional belief. Here he sets aside any practical justification of belief, and focuses instead on the evidentialist rule as a strictly epistemic principle. James's defense of passional belief here is not as precisely stated or sustained as one would have hoped. Still a clear argument may be developed from his remarks. I think the following reconstruction best represents his view.

What, James asks, is the best possible belief policy for us, given the fact that we seek the best possible evidence attainable for our beliefs? He observes that there are situations where it is necessary first to have faith that a proposition is true in order to arrive at the evidence for its truth. On the basis of this, James argues that in some cases it is irrational *on epistemic grounds themselves* to abide by the evidentialist rule. Here James challenges the evidentialist rule by examining the rule's own epistemic justification. Why is it, after all, as the evidentialists contend, that regarding beliefs for which evidence is appropriate one is required to consider his beliefs epistemically justified only if they are supported by adequate evidence? Clearly, James holds, it is because the better the evidence one has for a corrigible belief, the more likely it is that that belief is true. It is the desire that one's beliefs be true that motivates, and justifies, the requirement for adequate evidence. James makes the point as follows:

> The concrete man has but one interest—to be right. . . . The rules of the scientific game, burdens of proof, presumptions, *experimenta crucis,* complete inductions, and the like, are only binding on those who enter that game. As a matter of fact we all more or less do enter it, because it helps us to our end.[29]

The evidentialist rule is justified as a means for arriving at truth, and as such, James considers its applicability to be extensive but not universal. As a general rule it is useful in many instances in facilitating our arrival at true beliefs (often after considerable investigation, and by a series of investigators), and James grants that we ought to regularly abide by it in our scientific pursuits.[30] But—and this is the important point—if an individual *always* were to wait for adequate evidence, there would be certain propositions whose truth he would be forever debarred from acknowledging—namely, those propositions the evidence for which depends on the individual's belief. But if this is a consequence of the evidentialist rule, then the evidentialist rule is irrational. James claims:

> *A rule of thinking which would absolutely prevent me from acknowledging certain kinds of truth if those kinds of truth were really there, would be an irrational rule.*[31]

James reverts to the case of religion to illustrate how believing may be required for arriving at evidence. He claims that on the religious hypothesis, belief in God may be a necessary condition of His revealing Himself to us. James is here interested in expressing the view that since God is thought of as a personal God, He would be more likely to reveal Himself to individuals who appeal to His personal qualities by seeking Him out and desiring to know Him—that is to say, individuals who already show some measure of religious belief.[32] However this may be, pre-evidential religious belief may be appropriate on other grounds as well. It would seem that minimal or at least tentative religious belief is required for an individual to see objects or events as carrying religious significance, and hence as lending whatever empirical support there can be to the religious hypothesis. Thus faith would be necessary for the evidence in the case of religion, and thus it follows that if God did exist, pre-evidential belief would be justified.

In James's discussion of morality in "The Sentiment of Rationality" we find another case where he argues that belief is necessary for arriving at the evidence.[33] In considering whether this is a world in which moral value is objective, James argues that the only way this can be determined is by treating the hypothesis of the existence of moral value like a scientific one and testing it accordingly. We cannot test the hypothesis that morality is objective except by acting on it, James holds, and we cannot act as though the world were moral, or as though it were not, without the prior requisite belief. There are, of course, serious difficulties involved in the idea of using empirical consequences to test for the objectivity of moral value—for there is no reason to think that the empirical results of actions by themselves could establish the appropriateness of judging those actions in moral terms. Without prior establishment of the objective existence of values there would be no reason to interpret the consequences of actions as good or bad.

However this may be, we find that James's argument hinges on his now familiar idea that in order to act on a proposition one must first believe it, and this point also requires scrutiny in this context. While we have shown above that there are some significant instances where belief is required as a condition of action, still there seems little reason to think that this is so in many cases of acting in moral contexts. Indeed, it would seem that in some matters, in order to hedge against doing something seriously wrong, individuals are prepared to act rigorously, as though a particular moral principle applied, even when they are not sure or have no firm belief that it does. Thus, an individual's action against performing euthanasia on a terminally ill relative who requests it may not necessarily result from his belief that taking the life of another person in this situation is wrong (indeed, he may even be inclined to think that there are good reasons for it). Rather, he may feel that just in case such an action is wrong, and given that the stakes are so high, he wishes to avoid making such a serious mistake. Given situations like this, James is not convincing in his contention that the action required to test moral hypotheses must stem from relevant moral beliefs. We must conclude, then, that to answer the question of the existence of objective moral value, antecedent pre-evidential belief is not required.

A more promising instantiation of James's principle that faith is necessary for the evidence can be found in the context of empirical science. Some philosophers of science have argued, quite plausibly, that the acceptance of a scientific theory (at least provisionally and on some level) is necessary in order for evidence for that same theory to be collected.[34] The point here, similar to the case of evidence for religious belief, is that the investigators' beliefs themselves determine how the facts shall be interpreted, and thus to that extent determine what the evidence is and what it means. Pre-evidential faith in the theory is necessary in order for confirmation of the theory to be possible.

The preceding examples have been designed to show that James makes a valid point in his epistemic justification of faith—that there are some contexts in which it is clearly unreasonable to withhold belief in a proposition in advance of adequate evidence, since the only way one can obtain adequate evidence is by first holding that belief. The evidentialist rule is justified as a means of arriving at truth; yet in cases where faith is necessary for the evidence, the only way truth can be acknowledged is by violating the rule. Adherence to the evidentialist rule precludes the fulfillment of the purpose in terms of which the rule itself is justified. It is thus self-defeating and therefore irrational. As such, James vindicates his point that belief on passional grounds is both appropriate and necessary.

II

James's defense of the justifiability of faith has been the object of widespread and heated criticism. I have already answered what has been considered the serious objection that while James's arguments may justify action, they nevertheless fail to justify belief. I should now like to consider the broadest and most significant objection to James's view, viz., the claim that he is encouraging intellectual irresponsibility when he argues that passional grounds may justify belief. As a case in point, "The Will to Deceive" and "The Will to Make Believe" have been proposed as more appropriate titles for James's essay.[35] John Hick's remark about James is representative:

> The basic weakness of James's position is that it constitutes an unrestricted license for wishful thinking.[36]

So also is Dickinson Miller's:

> [James] took the worst weakness of the human mind, the bribery of the intelligence, and set it up as a kind of ideal.[37]

Quite obviously, James's proposal is thought to encourage willful irrationality and obduracy of belief. But it seems to me clear that this criticism is unjustified—that it misses entirely the subtlety of James's point. First, it ignores the fact that James rather narrowly delineates the circumstances under which belief on faith is legitimate. Second, it reflects a failure to appreciate the complexity and practical urgency of the situations in which we as believers may be placed. As I have shown, James does not recommend that the individual always hold beliefs on passional grounds, or even that he make a practice of doing so. It is only that he is justified in doing so in carefully specified kinds of situations. They are (1) when confronted with an intellectually undecidable genuine option; (2) when in a situation where belief in a fact is necessary for the existence of that fact; and (3) when in a situation where, given a proposition which is true, belief in that proposition is necessary for arriving at the evidence for its truth. In each of these three situations, there exists an individual who does not have adequate evidential grounds for belief, but for whom, James contends, belief would still be appropriate.

In this context, the critical question becomes whether a person would necessarily be intellectually irresponsible or in any way irrational if in these kinds of situations, on the basis of the principles James sets out, he held a belief on passional grounds. It is difficult to see why he would be. In the case in which belief in a proposition is necessary for arriving at the evidence for its truth, it is clearly self-defeating to withhold belief. In the case of the intellectually undecidable genuine option, as well as the situation in which faith in a fact is necessary for the existence of that fact, moral and prudential considerations may well override one's unfavorable epistemic position. That it may well be rational to use other than purely evidential considerations in justifying our beliefs becomes clear once it is recognized that we are not isolated intellects, judging in a vacuum whether to affirm or deny one proposition or another. Rather, we are individuals who must make our epistemic and other judgments in the context of the exigencies of practical life. James's point is that while the evidential criterion of justification is very important, still it would be wrong to extend it beyond its appropriate limits. It is not a call to frivolity or an encouragement of wishful thinking to insist that the weighing of evidence is not always the most appropriate action one can take in all of the situations of life. One's passional nature is not, for James, a repository of capriciousness. The sensitivity of James's point lies in its identification of passional beliefs with an individual's serious commitments. He puts his intentions clearly in the following remark:

> When you say to a man "don't guess," it can't mean, "don't come to a conclusion"—it can only mean, "be *serious*," "don't come to a silly, wanton, conclusion." The best pledge that my deliberations shall be serious is the participation in them of my passional nature.[38]

When all is considered, I think it is fair to conclude that James had no intention of supporting irrationally held beliefs; nor is there anything in the principles he provides which necessitates, or even encourages, wishful thinking. In his attempt to liberate his academic audiences from their incapacity for faith, his goal was achieved when he successfully set out principles under the guidance of which this could be accomplished.

James could rely on his audience's judiciousness, if not conservatisim, to guarantee that these principles not be abused in the concrete cases of their application. Still the point sympathetic to the critics which can be made is that, since James has not provided specific rules for the application of his principles in particular cases, he has left it possible for them to be misapplied and abused. It was not James's intention, of course, to provide a decision procedure for determining in any particular case whether and how his principles are applicable; nor is it clear whether it is even possible to construct one. Still, without such a decision procedure, it is possible for his principles to be overextended and used to justify irrationally held beliefs.

The preceding quotation from James concerning the seriousness of one's passional nature gives some indication of the problem. When in this passage James observes that passionally grounded beliefs are held with a great deal of seriousness, he does not quite answer the charge of his critics. Passionally held beliefs, because they are serious, are indeed insured against being capricious or frivolous. But frivolity is not the only way beliefs can go wrong. One may well be serious, indeed fanatically serious, about a belief and nevertheless be unjustified or irrational in holding it.

The possibility of abusing James's principles becomes particularly evident in cases where faith is necessary for the fact. In these cases, it will be remembered, the evidentialist rule may be overridden, and an inadequately evidenced belief may be justified on moral or prudential grounds. The other situation in which a belief's justification is given on the basis of moral and prudential considerations is the case of the intellectually undecidable genuine option, and the two situations may be fruitfully compared. In the genuine option situation the individual is *forced* to make a choice without sufficient evidence, and there is a high degree of importance in the choice he makes. These two facts together provide compelling justification for the individual's believing on passional grounds. Since some decision *must* be made, and the import of the decision is momentous, the individual is best off believing in accordance with his needs, desires, and interests. Comparing this with the situation where faith is necessary for the fact, we see that the choice situation is not so narrowly circumscribed. Since the option is not forced, the believer has the option of remaining sceptical. Moreover, the consequences of belief may not be particularly important. Given this as the context of his choice, if the individual does choose to hold a belief on inadequate evidence, in order to be justified in doing so it must be the case that the consequences of believing really are important enough to suspend the evidentialist rule.

But how is the subject to decide this? James leaves unspecified how important the consequences of belief must be, in non-forced options, before the principle that faith is necessary for the fact can justifiably be utilized. Perhaps the subject ought to believe on faith that he can make a ten-foot leap to save his life. Shall he believe on faith that he can make the leap, even when his life is not at stake, say, even for the sake of winning a bet? Does any goal, no matter how trivial, justify inadequately evidenced belief, if belief is necessary for achieving the goal? In pinpointing and describing the situation where faith is necessary for the fact, James makes a significant point in emphasizing the importance of belief as a phenomenon which may function to energize a person emotionally and spiritually. But insofar as the issue is whether such beliefs are rationally held, their epistemic relations—relations to evidence and the probability of their truth—must play a role in their assessment no less than their beneficial causal effects. James realizes this of course. But short of any detailed working out of the relation between these two diverse sets of considerations, it is not clear how important the consequences of one's belief must be in order to successfully override one's epistemic disadvantage.

Indeed, there is an additional problem. Does the individual actually need to believe in advance, say, that he can run a four-minute mile, or successfully complete a book, or succeed in business, in order to be able to do so? Certainly not in every case. But then, when is belief necessary to achieve the desirable consequences, and when can it be gone without? How can the subject tell? James leaves unspecified any criteria by which the subject can ascertain, *in advance* of belief, whether he actually is in a situation where faith is necessary for the fact.[39] Given this, the individual has no reliable method of determining when it is appropriate to go about the task of balancing the relevant epistemic and practical considerations. Perhaps in cases of uncertainty the reasonable individual would adopt a policy prescribing that when the consequences are so important that for the sake of increasing the probability of achieving them, one is justified in assuming himself to be in a situation where faith is necessary for the fact.

Given the complexity and uniqueness of choice situations, it is clearly too much to ask for any simple decision procedure that will automatically determine exactly when it is appropriate to believe in advance of adequate evidence. Nevertheless, without some guidelines for answering questions like the ones I have posed, it must be granted that in particular cases it is possible for James's principles to be abused in the interest of overzealousness, wishful thinking, and irrationality. The value of James's justification of faith lies not in particular details of its application, but rather in the insight with which he specifies the principles, and in a general way, the sorts of cases under which inadequately evidenced belief may be justified. This is sufficient to refute the evidentialist, and for James to have made his point.

6. A Pragmatic Theory of Truth

IN THE PHILOSOPHICAL TRADITION we find that there have been three major theories of truth: the correspondence, the coherence, and the pragmatic. James develops his pragmatic theory of truth as an alternative to the other two. As such, it is designed both to resolve the traditional problem of the nature of truth as well as to show the effectiveness of the pragmatic method as a way "of settling metaphysical disputes which might otherwise be interminable." [1] This theory represents James's most important contribution as a philosopher and lies at the heart of his philosophy. It follows naturally from his theories of meaning and his philosophy of mind. It is tied closely to his ethical theory and shares mutual influence with his view on the nature of reality.

Looking briefly at the historical background, we find that just as there are different theories of truth, there are differences among philosophers regarding that to which the predicate "true" is properly ascribed. Besides propositions, other candidates are, for example, beliefs, statements, ideas, and judgments. But in spite of their differences there is one important point of agreement among all three traditional theories. On each theory, to say that a proposition, belief, judgment, or whatever the bearer of truth-value, is true, is to designate a certain relation between it and something else.[2] At the very least, proponents of all three theories would concur on the common-sense level that a proposition is true if it agrees with reality. The theories differ, however, in their proposals as to how this notion of "agreement with reality" is to be understood. They provide competing analyses of the nature of that reality to which a true proposition must agree, and competing viewpoints as to the nature of that agreement.

On the traditional correspondence theory "agreement with reality" means "correspondence with the facts," and the "facts" are generally thought to be actual or hypothetical events or states of affairs. "Correspondence" is generally characterized in terms of the believer's ideas picturing, copying, or resembling the facts to which they refer, or the propositions expressing those ideas having a structural similarity to the facts to which they refer.[3] One of the most significant features of this theory is that facts are considered to objectively obtain, independently of any judgments made about them.

On the coherence theory in its traditional form, the truth of a proposition is determined not by its relation to independently existing facts, but rather by its relation to other propositions. "Reality" means Absolute Reality, and this is taken to be an all-inclusive, fully comprehensive, fully coherent system of propositions. Any single proposition or set of propositions, considered in isolation from the all-inclusive system in which it has its place, has only a partial degree of truth, and the degree to which any proposition is true is determined by the degree to which it coheres with the absolute system. Thus for the coherence theorist, the reality to which a true proposition must agree is the all-embracing Absolute, and the "agreement with reality" which determines a proposition's truth is constituted by the proposition's degree of coherence within the absolute system.[4]

James rejects both the correspondence and coherence theories. He rejects the former for its underlying model of mental activity as passive, non-interested, and non-evaluative. He rejects the latter for what he considers the abstract vacuity of its metaphysical foundations. But most importantly, James has a further, common objection .to both theories—one that is epistemological and methodological in character. His prime objection is that on both theories truth is conceived to exist, as he puts it, "ante rem," literally "prior to things." James uses the expression "truth ante rem" to refer to what contemporary philosophers would call a realist conception of truth—under which truth is seen to obtain prior to, and therefore independently of, human inquiry, experience, and belief. The correspondence theory involves a realist conception of truth because on this theory the truth of a proposition is determined by its relation to facts that exist independently of what anyone may believe about them. While on the coherence theory in its traditional form truth is tied to an idealist metaphysics, the concept of truth is nevertheless realistic in the sense that truth is seen to exist "ante rem." The truth of a proposition is taken to be determined by its relation to the absolute all-inclusive system, which is independent of human experience and belief. Indeed, adherents of the coherence theory go so far as to claim that the Absolute is unknowable by finite minds.

Taken in its broadest sense, James's objection to a realist conception of truth is that it is pragmatically meaningless. As has been shown in Chapter 3, James holds that it is only in terms of their concrete instantiations and consequences that abstract problems as well as their proposed solutions can be considered meaningful. As such, an adequate philosophical account of any subject must bring abstract questions down to their actual concrete differences in life. James holds that it is a failure of philosophical discernment to give an account of the nature of truth without regard for considerations of how individuals differentially react to claims they take to be true and those they take to be false; why they seek true rather than false beliefs; what makes persons call some judgments but not others true; what conditions they take to be important in establishing the truth of their claims; and what different consequences arise depending on whether a person's belief is true or false. James holds that any theory which ignores these parameters will result in a disembodied and artificial conception of truth—one without genuine meaning or value. The problem with the coherence and correspondence theories, according to James, is that they render the truth relation incapable of adequate articulation, and render the predicate "true" incapable of being reliably ascribed.[5]

The guiding idea behind James's theory, designed to correct for the deficiencies of the other two, is that truth is an experiential property. James contends that because truth is experiential, there is nothing about it which is inaccessible to us. As such, the concept of truth is capable of full and articulate description. Moreover, the fact that truth is experiential also guarantees that there is a reliable mechanism—the appeal to experience—for applying the concept in any particular case. We shall more fully examine the implications of these contentions below. The point to be made now is that James overcomes what he sees as the deficiencies of competing theories by constructing an analysis of truth in terms of the way true beliefs function in the lives of individuals. Truth, experientially or pragmatically understood, *is* nothing other than that which the subject *calls* true, or under the appropriate conditions would call true, on the basis of certain standards of acceptability.

I

It is important to note at the outset that James differentiates between three different sorts of beliefs, each with different criteria of truth. They are empirical beliefs, beliefs in logically necessary truths, and beliefs in what James calls the "postulates of rationality." The overriding emphasis in James's theory of truth is on the truth of empirical beliefs, and it is to these that we shall restrict our considerations.[6] Further, it is worth noting James's view of the object of truth ascriptions, since his position is unusual. He rejects the more traditional view that truth and falsity are most appropriately ascribed to propositions. Indeed, he rejects the idea of the "proposition," considering it merely a construction of philosophers. He holds it to be an ambiguous notion and one that severs truth from its concrete instantiations.[7] James considers truth-value properly ascribable only to such concrete embodiments as beliefs, statements, assertions, judgments, or ideas. For exegetical purposes we shall follow James as far as possible, in his reference to beliefs, judgments, and the like as the bearers of truth-value.

Though James never makes it explicit, one can readily discern that his theory of empirical truth is based solidly on his theory of meaning. As was shown in Chapter 3, the pragmatic meaning of a belief is constituted, first, by its predictive import and, second, by the consequences which follow in the life of the believer from the fact that it is held. Applying the theory of meaning to the theory of truth is instructive. To say that an empirical belief is pragmatically true is, first, to say something about its predictive import—namely, that its predictive import will be fulfilled. For James, this means that under the appropriate conditions the empirical consequences which logically follow from that which is believed will in fact occur; or minimally, that there will be no experiential ground to expect that they would not occur. This is the "verifiability" condition of truth. Second, to say that a belief is pragmatically true is to say something about the consequences in the life of the believer which result from his holding that belief—namely, that they are satisfactory. This is the "satisfactoriness" condition. We shall examine each of these in turn.

James begins his analysis of truth with the notion of verification. He characterizes the verification of a belief in thoroughly experiential terms—describing it by reference to the idea's "motor and ideational associates." [8] The verification of a belief occurs when the actions and other ideas associated with it follow an acceptable pattern of succession; when, within the individual's experience, "the connexions and transitions come to [him] from point to point as being progressive, harmonious, satisfactory." [9] There are passages in which James claims that the truth of a belief is the same as the actual process of its verification, and suggests that no belief could be true unless it had *already* been verified in experience.[10] But these are overstatements on his part. The point he is actually out to make is the more restricted one that truth is to be analyzed in terms of "verifiability."

James uses the notion of "verifiability" in his own way. Normally, the "verifiability" of a proposition is intended by philosophers to refer to its capability in principle of being *either* proved *or* confuted by experience; and to say that a proposition is verifiable is to allow that it is equally capable, in principle, of disproof as it is of proof. But when James refers to the verifiability of a belief, he is referring only to the positive of these two alternatives. On James's view, an individual's belief is "verifiable" for him over a given period of time as long as it is capable of being increasingly confirmed in his experience over that period of time. It is worth emphasizing that on this view a belief is not verifiable simpliciter. Its verifiability is defined in light of the concrete situations of particular believers, and it may change over person and over time. Beliefs that are verifiable in the experience of one person may not be verifiable in the different experience of another; and beliefs that are verifiable in one person's experience over one span of time might later, in his experience, be disconfirmed.[11] This temporal and personal relativity of James's concept of verifiability has important implications for his fully articulated theory of truth, as we shall see below. Let us simply note now that with James's concept of verifiability he begins his theory of truth from an utterly subjective and personal starting point: each individual with his own set of beliefs verifiable in the context of his own possibly idiosyncratic experience. As we shall see, in his fully developed account of truth James attempts to show how objectively true beliefs are possible though built on such a subjective foundation.

In order that the subject's belief be verifiable, on James's view, he need not actually be acquiring direct sensible confirmation of it—the evidence may be indirect. Thus, an individual may verify that he has sufficient gasoline in his automobile, for example, not by looking into the tank, but by checking the gauge. Indeed, James holds that the evidence for the truth of a belief commonly consists solely in the fact that the believer has had no experiences which disconfirm it. The subject may verify that he has sufficient gasoline by embarking on his trip and observing whether he manages to reach his destination. Frequently, a true belief's agreement with reality, James claims, "will only mean the negative fact that nothing contradictory from the quarter of that reality comes to interfere with the way in which our ideas guide us elsewhere." [12] He holds that any experiences which indirectly confirm the belief, or which provide the subject with no reason to doubt the belief, which remain congruous with the experiential predictive import of the proposition believed, count toward the proposition's verifiability and provide evidence for its truth. In *Pragmatism* James gives an example to illustrate his position:

> Take, for instance, yonder object on the wall. You and I consider it to be a "clock," altho no one of us has seen the hidden works that make it one. We let our notion pass for true without attempting to verify. . . . We *use* it as a clock, regulating the length of our lecture by it. The verification of the assumption here means its leading to no frustration or contradiction. Verif*iability* of wheels and weights and pendulum is as good as verification.[13]

Regarding a belief's predictive import, it is James's pragmatic, functionalist standpoint that leads him to analyze truth in terms of verifiability rather than actual verification. When the subject holds a belief that he finds in an increasing number of trials not to be disconfirmed, he has no reason not to act upon it. But if this is the case, and given James's view that the function of belief is propitious action, then the belief is perfectly acceptable. Pragmatically, then, it must count as true. As James observes in *Essays in Radical Empiricism*, "what more could we have *done* at those moments even if the later verification comes complete?" [14]

James's use of verifiability as a central criterion of truth derives from his principle that truth be analyzed exclusively by reference to actual or possible experience. Verifiability is analyzed exclusively according to the way in which the individual's belief is or could be *experienced* as verifiable—by the absence of discontinuities in his experience, the lack of jolts, surprises, or inexplicably abrupt transitions. Furthermore, for a belief to remain verifiable it must be increasingly confirmed in the individual's experience. Over an increasing amount of time and opportunity for confutation, none occurs. Again, the idea here is that the individual ascertains the truth of his belief exclusively by appeal to his experience—using one experience to test the veridicality of another. Eschewing any reference to objects existing independently of experience, James posits that that which is external to a belief, against which it is measured as true or false, is simply the future experience of the believer himself:

> The only *real* guarantee we have against licentious thinking is the circumpressure of experience itself, which gets us sick of concrete errors, whether there be a transempirical reality or not.[15]

In sum, there are two points of particular importance concerning the verifiability condition. First, James's recognition (in spite of several critics) that there must be a criterion external to a given belief by which to test the veridicality of that belief. This is in order to avoid subjectivism.[16] Second, his insistence that such a criterion must come from within the texture of experience itself.[17]

The second element in the meaning of truth for

James involves the consequences in the life of the believer which follow from his holding true beliefs. James refers to these consequences by using the idea of "satisfactoriness." "Satisfactoriness" in James's philosophy is a rich concept, embodying a family of notions, each related to certain sorts of consequential value which the belief has for the person who holds it. James also uses the notion of a belief's satisfactoriness in a more restrictive way, referring to the positive feeling tone that occurs in the process of verifying it. The feelings that subjectively constitute a belief's verifiability—of fulfillment of expectation, smooth experiential transition, and the like—embody feelings of positive value or satisfaction. These satisfactions are not extrinsic to a belief's verifiability, but rather are part and parcel of it. This notion of satisfactoriness as embedded in the verifiability experience introduces a valuational element into the notion of verifiability. The result is an expansion of epistemological discussion, having far-reaching implications regarding the separability of the normative and the descriptive. If verifiability is inextricably value-laden, and if truth depends on verifiability, then truth and the ascertainment of truth are value-laden as well.

However interesting this may be, the concept of satisfactoriness as embedded in verifiability is not the concept which plays the major role in James's theory. Rather, it is the satisfactory *use* which can be made of verifiable beliefs which most captures James's attention. The most important valuational aspect of James's theory of truth is the idea that in order for a belief to be true it must be "useful," "adaptive," "serviceable," "workable," "satisfying," or "expedient." To be true, a belief must indeed fit realities—it must be verifiable and enable the believer to make correct predictions about any of his relevant future experience. But that by itself is not enough. "The *truest* fit" for a belief, James emphasizes, "is the richest fit." [18] Those beliefs are truest which not only enable the subject to predict his experiences, but also enable him most effectively to adapt to or change his environment, and most inclusively fulfill his purposes and answer his interests.

In holding that the satisfactoriness of a belief is the key to its truth, James takes the notion of truth as agreement with reality and thoroughly transforms it to meet the requirements of his own point of view. Ordinarily, one would expect the notion of "agreement with reality" to be analyzable independently of reference to any value that may be derived from holding true beliefs. It might well be granted that holding beliefs which are true, as a matter of fact, ordinarily does lead to beneficial results; for the more accurately one represents the facts, the better one will be enabled to deal with them. But most would hold that the consequences of believing truly have no effect whatever on whether the beliefs are true at the outset.

All of this changes in James's hands. In *Pragmatism* he is careful to grant that "agreement with reality" is the dictionary definition of truth.[19] But, against the correspondence theory, James holds that to agree with reality is not to copy it or otherwise represent it in thought. Indeed, in a subtle change of reference James places the locus of agreement with reality not on the belief, but on the believer.

> To "agree" in the widest sense with a reality *can only mean to be guided either straight up to it or into its surroundings, or to be put into such working touch with it as to handle either it or something connected with it better than if we disagreed.*[20]

A belief "agrees with" reality if it leads the believer to a position of being "in agreement with" reality rather than conflicting with it—that is to say, if it leads him to a facilitation of the fulfillment of his demands by accounting for that reality and fruitfully relating to it.[21]

This notion of truth as satisfactory belief is one that is fundamentally valuational—indeed, if we accept James's ethical theory, one that is moral in character. As the satisfaction of demand provides the essence of goodness in James's ethical theory, it also provides the essence of truth in his epistemology. James declares

plainly in *Pragmatism* that "truth is *one species of good.*" [22]
True beliefs are created by the subject in the process of
constructing that interpretation of his experience
which will best fulfill his demands, given the limitations
set by the empirical conditions under which he finds
himself.

James has set up the foundations of his theory of
truth in his logically prior view of the teleological function of conceptualization and belief. As we have seen in
Chapter 2, James holds that human interest provides
the principle by which the subject selectively attends to
incoming sensations and determines in each case which
groups of sensations he shall discriminate as a single
object. Further, human interest determines what he
conceives to be the essential nature of each object, and
what beliefs he shall hold about it. This selectivity is
utilized for the sake of successful action. The function
of thought is to help fulfill the believer's interests. In
line with this, the acceptability or truth of a belief is
determined by how well it succeeds in achieving this.

Using as a key concept in his analysis the notion of
satisfactoriness — with its essential reference to the feelings of the subject — James has rendered his theory
susceptible to the common criticism that it is far too
subjectivistic to be an adequate account of truth.
Against James, it may be held, first, that there is little
reason to think that the subject's feelings or the satisfaction of the subject's demands can give any indication
of objective facts. Second, it may be held that even if
some subjective feelings did carry epistemic import,
James's theory would still founder. For it fails to offer a
mechanism for distinguishing between those subjective
states that provide objective information and those that
do not.[23]

Regarding the first point, it is a mistake to think that
because James's notion of satisfactoriness involves reference to the feelings of the subject, it is therefore defined *exclusively* in terms of those feelings. We shall
consider this in detail shortly. The second criticism is
more telling, however. If we grant that certain ways in

which a belief may be satisfactory are relevant to its truth while other ways are not, we find that James does not adequately account for this fact. Indeed, occasionally James suggests that almost any sort of satisfactoriness whatever which comes from holding a belief is relevant to its truth. In *Pragmatism*, for example, he makes the unlikely suggestion that the true is the "expedient in almost any fashion." [24] Elsewhere he proposes to test the truth of a belief by a single quantitative criterion — in terms of the "completer sum of satisfactions" the belief brings.[25] Against this view, it would seem far more reasonable to allow only certain sorts of satisfactory consequences to count as relevant to the truth of a belief. If a particular empirical belief satisfied a fantasy, or was, say, aesthetically or spiritually enriching, but was one which contradicted other well-grounded beliefs, or was one which led to unfulfilled predictions, then that belief would likely be false. The belief in this case would be satisfactory in some ways, but it would not be satisfactory in ways relevant to its truth.

While at times James seems to intend any sort of satisfactoriness as relevant in the assessment of truth, this is by no means his considered view. While he characterizes truth in terms of the fulfillment of the subject's interests, it is not the fulfillment of any interests whatsoever that guarantees truth. James does not envision the subject renouncing objective and rigorous criteria in deciding what to believe. Factors pertinent to an individual's formation of beliefs are his demands for rationality, consistency, clarity, theoretical elegance, scientific objectivity, and the like.[26] Moreover, to be true, a belief must enable the subject to account for and understand his incoming experience, and it must do this without undermining previously formed beliefs which he is not prepared to renounce, and without violating any necessary truths which form part of his conceptual scheme. It is only after these conditions are met, James holds, that exclusively idiosyncratic or personal demands may legitimately count toward the acceptability of any belief.[27] Indeed, James recognizes the

fact that few of the believer's demands of whatever sort
will be satisfied if he refuses to take the hard facts of
the experiential flux into account.[28]

Satisfactoriness, it may be noted, is a dispositional
property and not an occurrent one. It would be foolish
to think that because a jackhammer or chainsaw is a
useful tool, that it is useful under all conditions (for
example when trying to drive a nail). It would be
equally naive to assume that if a belief is satisfactory it
will thereby invariably facilitate the fulfillment of the
interests of the believer. A belief, no matter how satisfactory, must minimally be relevant to the believer's
situation actually to be useful. James explains that we
store our "extra truths"—those not presently relevant—in our memories and reference books, to be
brought to work again when appropriate to the conditions at hand.[29] Furthermore, even when relevant, a
true belief will be useful only if the believer is capable
of acting on it, only if he is not constrained, for example, by physical or emotional restrictions.

This understanding of "satisfactoriness" as the dispositional, functional usefulness of a belief is one that
integrates and renders comprehensive the two major
constituents of James's theory of truth. The co-
occurrence of the satisfactoriness and verifiability conditions is explained when we consider that it is only
verifiable beliefs which characteristically will be capable
of satisfying the believer. A belief that is not verifiable
will not in itself (that is to say, unless accidentally or
coincidentally) help him deal more expediently with
the experiential world. It can only be inexpedient. As
the pragmatic meaning of a belief consists in its predictive import and the consequences which follow from
the fact that it is held, an unverifiable empirical belief
characteristically will be such that the consequences
entailed by that belief will not occur, and the consequences in the subject's life of holding that belief will
consist mainly in the disappointment of his expectations. Given the inaccuracy of the subject's predictions,
any actions he performs on the basis of his belief will

likely be inappropriate at some point to what does in fact occur, and consequently at some point those actions will prove to be maladaptive. In sum, the satisfactoriness of an empirical belief involves its verifiability because satisfactoriness is dependent upon objective conditions, conditions grounded in the nature of the empirical world which those beliefs are about. On James's view, the satisfactoriness which functions as a condition of truth *must derive from the successful reference of the idea to a verifiable object:*

> [The truth of a man's beliefs] consists . . . in such a working on the part of the beliefs as may bring the man into satisfactory relations with objects *to which these latter point.*[30]

> The pragmatist . . . asks what such "agreement" [holding between ideas and reality, such that the ideas are true of that reality] may mean in detail. He finds first that the ideas must point to or lead toward *that* reality and no other, and then that the pointings and leadings must yield satisfaction as their result.[31]

A lack of appreciation of the link between satisfactoriness and verifiability has led to erroneous criticisms of James's theory. G. E. Moore, for instance, in an objection characteristic of the response of many philosophers to James, states that on one possible interpretation James is claiming that all satisfactory beliefs are true. As a counterexample to this Moore imagines a man who misses a train because of a false belief about the accuracy of his watch.[32] He points out that if it were to turn out that the train was destroyed in a railway accident, then the man's belief would indeed have turned out to be satisfactory—because it saved his life—even though it was false.

It should now be clear just how Moore misunderstands James's point. He interprets James as holding that any consequences whatever contribute to determining the truth-value of a belief. But in Moore's example, the fact that the train crashed is something which could never be inferred or predicted by any belief the subject might have in the accuracy of his watch. And that is why these consequences are irrelevant to the belief's truth-value. James does not count as capable of fulfilling the satisfactoriness condition consequences extrinsic to the belief's own meaning, which merely happen to occur, coincidentally, or fortuitously, when the individual holds the belief. Reverting to James's metaphor of beliefs as instruments, it would be a non sequitur to infer that a particular tool is a good one because on the day one used it, one happened also to win a lottery jackpot. Similarly, James would consider it absurd to hold that a belief about a watch is true merely because it kept one off a train that happened to crash.

II

A singularly important consequence of positing satisfactoriness and verifiability as the joint constituents of truth is that, if James's analysis is successful, he will have rendered truth describable exclusively by reference to what human beings can experience. In order to provide the most concrete analysis possible, James uses as the starting point for his theory the viewpoint of the single individual. Truth in the first instance, for James, is truth for the individual. This renders truth relative to each individual, and, within the life of the person, relative to the time during which the belief in question remains unconfuted and functions satisfactorily. This means that on the individual level, the truth of a belief may be severely restricted—the belief may function adequately only for that individual, and only within a very small range of experiences. James sees that to provide the most concrete possible account of truth, he must begin his analysis from the standpoint of the individual and the beliefs that work for him.

It is also evident to James that more needs to be done if his account is to achieve all that a theory of truth should. James recognizes that no analysis of truth can stand as adequate unless it can explain and provide grounding for the fact that truth is objective, and not individual, personal, or idiosyncratic. He takes it as his goal, then, to establish the objectivity of true beliefs while starting from only the individual's subjective "truths," and without appeal to anything outside experience. He attempts to achieve this by developing a doctrine of degrees of truth—one that begins from relative truth for a solitary individual at a particular time, and leads ultimately to the notion of an ideally perfect objective absolute truth, with intermediary stages being a set of progressively more objective judgments made by a community of inquirers.[33] It is to this doctrine that we shall now turn.

In Chapter 4, when we examined James's ethical theory, we saw that he begins with the experiences and judgments of a single individual and uses these as the basis for generating criteria for making objective judgments. There is a remarkable and instructive parallelism between James's epistemology and his ethics. His use of satisfactoriness and verifiability as the criteria for ascribing truth enables him to maintain an exclusively experiential standard of truth in much the same way that the satisfaction of demand in his ethical theory provides an exclusively experiential criterion of moral value. Recalling his ethical theory, James argues that in the case of a "moral solitude" an individual will take to be good whatever most inclusively satisfies his demands. He argues further that in this situation there can be no other test for what is good independent of what the individual thinks is good, and that, therefore, one's taking something to be good is in fact what constitutes its goodness. James then goes on to contend that in a world of many individuals, the constitution of morality, while more complicated, is not in any essential way different from that of a moral solitude. It is merely a derivation from the case of a single individual, with no important new principles being invoked. Moral value is still constituted by the satisfaction of demand; the difference now is simply that not merely the conflicting demands within one individual, but also the conflicting demands among individuals need to be balanced and harmonized in order to arrive at the best possible moral result. Thus the judgment of the solitary individual is the conceptual starting point of James's ethical theory—and so it is also for his theory of truth. In *The Meaning of Truth* James has us imagine a solitary individual in the context of deciding which beliefs to hold:

> Can we imagine a man absolutely satisfied with an idea and with all its relations to his other ideas and to his sensible experiences, who should yet *not* take its content as a true account of reality? The *matter* of the true is thus absolutely identical with the matter of the satisfactory.[34]

James's point here is that if an individual uses all the tests for truth available to him and on the best evidence comes to the conclusion that a proposition at hand is true, it is utterly senseless, from within the context of the experience of *that* individual at *that* time, to hold that his belief is not true. For within that experience frame there is no way in which this could be discovered, and hence it would be a meaningless postulation. Truth, pragmatically understood, is that which is judged to be true, given the use of appropriate tests, and nowhere is this clearer than when truth is seen within the context of a single individual seeking to formulate and justify his beliefs.

In the moral solitude, the good is that which the individual takes to be good, given the nature of the demands of his that call to be satisfied, and the material at hand which can be used to satisfy them. In the "epistemic solitude," as it may be called, the true is that which the individual takes to be true, given the nature of the purposes and interests he seeks to fulfill and the character of the experiential flux in which he seeks to fulfill them.[35]

In the ethics, James moves from a moral solitude to a plurality of individuals each seeking to have his demands satisfied. He extends his ethical theory from a solitary individual to a group by using the principle that conflicting demands between different individuals should be satisfied as fully as possible. If we act on principles of integration, harmonization, and inclusivity of the satisfaction of demand, we will arrive at a progressively more objective ethical arrangement. It becomes progressively more objective in the sense that more and more people would be willing to consent to it—there would be continually fewer complaints. As such, there would be progressively less possibility of replacing the current arrangement with a better (i.e., more inclusively satisfactory) one.

A parallel principle lies behind James's theory of truth. The starting point of the theory lies in the personal, restricted, relative "truths" in the limited experience of single individuals. From this beginning James ultimately aims for an explanation of fully objective truth. The mechanism linking subjective and objective truth is his doctrine that truth admits of degrees. First, James holds that the verifiability of true beliefs admits of degrees. If, for a certain period of time, an empirical belief is increasingly confirmed although later experience confutes it, or if the belief is increasingly confirmed in the experience of one person but not in the experience of another, then that belief is only relatively verifiable, verifiable only within certain limits, or only to a certain degree.[36] Second, James holds that the satisfactoriness of true beliefs admits of degrees: it is possible for a belief to be satisfactory for only a certain limited period of time or limited number of persons.[37]

In order to continue to be true, on James's view, an individual's belief must withstand confutation by future experience. The more extensively (both over person and over time) an account of the empirical world survives the test of being satisfactory and verifiable, the truer it will be. As an individual's experience accumulates, there is progressively more data for which his beliefs must account; and if he is to maintain a satisfactory relationship with his environment—to fulfill his purposes in the context of making successful predictions—his set of beliefs must become more complex, refined, and capable of accounting for a continually more inclusive range of facts. Yet the breadth of experience required for formulating beliefs which will remain satisfactory and verifiable for any reasonable length of time is beyond the possibility of achievement by a single individual. The individual's truths, continually subject to future confutation, would not hold up well under the enormous multiplicity of future experience if he could not draw on the experiences of others—thereby widening, by proxy, his own point of view. James envisions the situation as follows:

> You accept my verification of one thing, I yours of another. We trade on each other's truth.[38]

> We exchange ideas; we lend and borrow verifications, get them from one another by means of social intercourse. All truth thus gets verbally built out, stored up, and made available for everyone.[39]

James's view, then, is that truths develop in a community. Individuals together, by means of shared knowledge and investigation, pool their experience, and the group develops sets of beliefs having progressively greater degrees of truth. In this way the members of the community are progressively better able to account for and anticipate a greater number and variety of experiences. As such, they come to hold beliefs which are progressively more objective in that they increasingly transcend limited or partial points of view. Just as in his ethical theory James postulates progressively more inclusive ethical arrangements culminating in an ideal system that will not be superseded by anything better (for there will be no complaints), in the theory of truth he postulates belief systems of ever-increasing degrees of truth, culminating in an ideal end-point that will not be superseded by a better set of beliefs (for there will be no confuting experiences). This James calls "absolute truth." [40]

James's notion of absolute truth raises its own set of

questions, which we shall examine presently. But first it will help to reiterate and clarify the grounding and context of this notion, in terms of the main lines of his theory. Finding it necessary to reject as meaningless any realist notion of truth, under which truth is held to obtain independently of experience, James introduces his notion of absolute truth. James posits absolute truth as a concept which is describable in exclusively experiential terms but which also is designed to meet the requirement that truth be objective, in the sense that it be independent of the accidents of personal and idiosyncratic experience and judgment. James thinks that he can meet this requirement and still avoid trans-experiential truth by analyzing absolute truth by reference to the relative truths of individuals and groups of individuals. For James the notion of relative truth is an exclusively experiential one, and so he sees absolute truth—as the ideal limit on a scale of ever-increasing degrees of relative truth—as thoroughly experiential also.

Does James succeed in articulating a conception of absolute truth which is both fully experiential and fulfills the requirement of objectivity? The answer to this question is more complex than might have been anticipated: examination reveals that there are several distinct meanings or levels discernible in "absolute truth" as James uses it. James himself makes no distinctions among these, yet their implications are importantly different.

On one level, James appears to intend his concept of absolute truth to be quite narrow in meaning. As a relative truth is a belief which in fact *is* not confuted in the experience of a person or persons, in some passages James restricts himself to the point that an absolute truth is a truth which in fact *will never be* confuted. At the extreme, this may mean no more than that a belief may be absolutely true if there is no opportunity of testing it. Thus, in *Essays in Radical Empiricism*, James claims that if the world were to come to an end the beliefs which were held at the moment the world ended would be absolutely true: for by hypothesis there would be no future possibility of bringing to bear data to confute them.

> The immediate experience in its passing is always "truth," practical truth, *something to act on*, at its own movement. If the world were then and there to go out like a candle, it would remain truth absolute and objective, for it would be "the last word," would have no critic, and no one would ever oppose the thought in it to the reality intended.[41]

This passage strikingly brings out James's view of the relationship between truth-value and confutability, yet there is little doubt that here he overstates and over-simplifies his case. In analyzing what it might mean for a belief to be one that will not be confuted, it will not help to focus on cases where there is no future in which the confutation can be carried out. For if there is to be no future, and if a belief's truth-value relies on a future experiential test, then both truth and falsity would be impossible. Indeed, elsewhere James makes much of the fact that if the world were to end, at the final moment all beliefs would then be pragmatically meaningless, since they would have no future conse-quences.[42] We must conclude, then, that while James succeeds in preserving an experiential standpoint when conceiving of absolute truth in this first way, he does not preserve truth's objectivity. For under the condi-tions and assumptions specified, a belief that counts as true would by the same token count as meaningless.

Clearly, the more significant question regarding absolute truth is whether, *assuming a future*, the belief in question would eventually be confuted, and what the implications of this would be. Indeed, this is the issue toward which James aims on a second, and deeper, meaning attached to the notion of absolute truth. On this level, by "absolute truth" James is pointing to those beliefs that eventually will be accepted by the commu-nity. In a passage reminiscent of Peirce,[43] James gives the following characterization in *The Meaning of Truth*:

> Truth absolute, [the pragmatist] says, means an ideal set of formulations towards which all opinions may in the long run of experience be expected to converge.[44]

The same idea appears in *Pragmatism*:

> The "absolutely" true, meaning what no farther experi-
> ence will ever alter, is that ideal vanishing-point towards
> which we imagine that all our temporary truths will some
> day converge.[45]

The point of importance in this characterization of
absolute truth is that it is seen to be constituted by
comprehensive intersubjective agreement. If all were to
come to agree about a proposition, there would be
none for whom it would count as false. Insofar as there
would be no one to reject it, then, pragmatically it
would be absolutely true.

While this second meaning of absolute truth, like
James's first, has the advantage of remaining within
experiential parameters, we must nevertheless conclude that it also fails to preserve truth's objectivity.
There is nothing self-contradictory about all persons
agreeing to a proposition that is nevertheless false,
even if its falsity were never discovered. Nor, on the
other hand, is it inconsistent, or even implausible, to
hold that a proposition may be absolutely true even
though some may fail to believe it.[46] James cannot
preserve the objectivity required of truth if he defines
absolute truth in terms of those beliefs about which
there is (or will be) comprehensive intersubjective
agreement. For the upshot of human opinion, however
rational and objective it *may* be, could quite possibly be
otherwise.

It might be held that merely to assert this position
against James is not to refute him, but only to express a
competing set of philosophical assumptions. There are
two that are especially relevant. One is the idea that it
makes sense to separate the existence of truth from the
concrete beliefs in which it is embodied. The other is
that objectivity is a quality which obtains independently
of the way beliefs are tested and the agreements we
come to regarding them. While it is true that James has
developed his case by denying these assumptions, one
nevertheless finds that he is at the same time commit-

ted to them, as we shall presently show. Moving to the deepest and most considered level of meaning in James's conception of absolute truth, we find that he goes beyond reference to intersubjective agreement and actual belief.

On this sense of absolute truth, James appeals to the idea of a future consensus, but he is careful to qualify and restrict what he means by it. He shows himself to be well aware of the plurality and diversity, as well as the non-rational motives, of human belief, and hence he does not propose a notion of absolute truth which involves the postulation of agreement between all persons. James recognizes that "men do exist who are 'opinionated,' in the sense that their opinions are self-willed." [47] He recognizes that some opinions are better than others, that believers differ in their sagacity, or in the breadth and type of experience upon which their judgments are founded. He holds that beliefs which are progressively more satisfactory are achieved only by the interaction of intelligent, informed, and impartial individuals attempting together to find the best possible account of their experience. [48] On this notion of absolute truth, agreement by itself is not the determining factor. What is significant, rather, is the agreement among only those individuals who are competent and in a position to make the relevant knowledge claims.

As universal agreement is not necessary for absolute truth, it is not sufficient either. In *The Meaning of Truth* James allows that it is possible for the beliefs which are the objects of universal intersubjective agreement to be false:

> No pragmatist needs to *dogmatize* about the consensus of opinion in the future being right—he need only *postulate* that it will probably contain more of truth than anyone's opinion now. [49]

To sum the matter up, while the notion of consensual agreement is important at the deepest level of James's concept of absolute truth, its role in his theory is less straightforward than it first appears. In the search for truth we engage in an intersubjective process of inquiry where we test the satisfactoriness of any belief by appeal to our own experience and the experiences of others which are relevant to our own. James predicts that as a matter of fact the more we come to agree on an issue, the closer we will come to absolute truth, but not because absolute truth is defined in terms of agreement. This is due, rather, to the obvious but highly important fact that the better the explanation of our experience, the more extensively we will agree with regard to it. And it is this "regulative notion"[50] of the most satisfactory possible account which constitutes James's most sophisticated conception of absolute truth. On this conception, absolute truth is not dependent upon beliefs which presently are held or those which will be held, since any present or future belief would be absolutely false if there were possible an alternative belief which could provide a better account of experience.[51]

Does James's characterization of absolute truth in this third sense preserve objectivity? I think we may conclude that it does. As the ideal end-point of inquiry, as a set of beliefs which cannot conceivably be improved upon, absolute truth must be considered fully objective—for there is no conceivable alternative of greater objectivity against which it could be found wanting.

Does this conception of absolute truth also meet the second requirement—that of being exclusively experiential? On this count James's analysis is less successful. This can be seen if we consider that absolute truth is held by James to be the ideally best possible account of experience. The most significant point in this regard is the fact that as the ideally best account, absolute truth is not dependent upon opinions actually held. Thus James believes that certain propositions are absolutely true at the present time even if as a community of inquirers, within the context of our limited experience, we have no reason to accept them. James makes this point when he claims that absolute truth has "powers of retroactive legislation." [52]

It is precisely this point that causes problems in James's analysis. The problem comes from the fact that whatever goes to make an account of experience the best possible one is something which is determined independently of whether that account actually is or will be believed. For that matter, absolute truth here is considered to be independent of any experiences the subject may have which might cause him to hold one belief over another. But the notion that an idea can be true though possibly never recognized as such is one which is inadmissible on James's own experientialism. It must be concluded, then, that James preserves his experientialism only nominally when, on this final conception of absolute truth, he characterizes it in terms of human beliefs. The hypothetical and normative notion of absolute truth as the best possible account of experience, an account which is retroactively true even before it is held, renders otiose reference to any beliefs which are actually held. As we have seen, the appeal to an account which is the best possible one is required if James is to preserve the objectivity of absolute truth. But the undesirable yet unavoidable consequence of this is that James must forsake his experientialism.

To sum up our considerations on absolute truth, we must conclude that in none of his conceptions of it does James fully achieve his end. The criterion of objectivity and the principle of experience are necessarily at odds. Objectivity requires that truth be analyzed in terms of the best possible account of experience, and there is no way in which this can be characterized in exclusively experiential terms. The use of only experiential predicates can yield at most an account of experience which is *accepted as* the best, and this is not sufficient.

III

James's analysis of truth in terms of the experiences, activities, and beliefs of subjects is radically different from traditional approaches to this issue. Typically, philosophers have been concerned with the meaning of the concept of truth, and have treated truth as a property whose nature is specifiable independently of any reference to the individual subject and his beliefs. The processes involved in the individual's verification of his beliefs, the grounds upon which he makes truth ascriptions, the causal antecedents of acquiring truths, or the results which follow upon his holding true beliefs are generally thought to be extrinsic to the nature of truth per se. While such phenomena are *contingently* related to a belief's being true, they do not form part of what it *means* for the belief to be true. But James appears to be concerned with just these sorts of contingencies. He outlines the numerous psychological, anthropological, and sociological facts that characterize the way truth functions in human life, as well as the concrete value truth has for individuals. In *Pragmatism*, for instance, James says of his theory that it is "a *genetic* theory of what is meant by truth." [53] In emphasizing the psychological import of his view, he reports that pragmatists "have only sought to trace exactly why people follow [truth] and always ought to follow it." [54] In *The Meaning of Truth*, moreover, James gives the following description of truth:

> "What is truth *known-as*? What does its existence stand for in the way of concrete goods?" . . . The true is the opposite of whatever is instable, of whatever is practically disappointing, of whatever is useless, of whatever is lying and unreliable, of whatever is unverifiable and unsupported, of whatever is inconsistent and contradictory, of whatever is artificial and eccentric, of whatever is unreal in the sense of being of no practical account.[55]

Remarks such as these would appropriately occur, it seems, only in an account concerned with empirical facts relating to the function and value of truth in human life. But they seem hardly relevant to a philosophical analysis of its meaning. One might ask, then, whether by invoking the sorts of considerations he does, James shows a failure to recognize that which is central, or at least traditional, in the philosophical question of truth. If James's theory were limited to exclusively empirical considerations concerning the role and value of truth in human life, it might well be interesting and illuminating, but it would fail to deal with the issues one reasonably may expect a philosophical theory of truth to address.

One commentator on James, A. J. Ayer, relies on this distinction between the empirical correlates of truth and its meaning. He contends that James is not concerned with articulating a formal concept of truth but finds significant only the empirical question of how we go about making truth ascriptions. Thus, Ayer holds, it would have "cost James nothing" to have conceded that there is a legitimate formal concept of truth. James need simply have noted that this formal concept of truth is logically independent of the way in which "truth" is ascribed to our factual beliefs. Hence it would not be relevant to the kind of analysis he was offering.[56]

While it seems clear that Ayer is correct to distinguish the truth of a proposition from its being acceptable or accepted as true, nevertheless it must be recognized that this is not a distinction which James could consistently make. Moreover, James would most certainly reject the implied suggestion that the analysis of the formal concept of truth, as contrasted to concrete ascriptions of truth, constitutes the real philosophical concern. As we have seen in Chapter 3, James's theory of pragmatic meaning is one which ties the meaning of a concept to the actual empirical conditions of its use. While James holds that it may make sense in limited contexts to consider the abstract analytic meanings of concepts, he does not consider the severance of a concept from the conditions of its application to be useful for arriving at philosophical conclusions. The concept of truth, for James, is a summarizing abstraction from particular "truths." That is to say, it names a relation which can be fully articulated only by reference to actual or possible true beliefs—beliefs which concretely function as true in the subject's life.[57] We must conclude, then, that Ayer has misunderstood James on this important point. It would have cost James considerably to treat his pragmatic account of truth as addressing a question different from the traditional one. For this would be contrary to the purport of his theory of meaning, and would rob his theory of truth of most of its philosophical significance.

Another James scholar, H. S. Thayer, articulates the philosophical implications involved in grounding the pragmatic meaning of truth in concrete conditions. In a recent and perspicuous account, Thayer gives a full portrayal of the rich and complex way in which pragmatic considerations function in determining the meaning of truth for James.[58] His appreciation of the fact that James does address the issue of the meaning of truth (its pragmatic meaning) constitutes a significant advance over Ayer's analysis. Indeed, it would seem appropriate to take this approach even further. Thayer shows correctly that James is attempting to give a detailed specification of the way true beliefs function in human life, and that he is not concerned with an abstract analysis of the concept for its own sake. Further, he shows that James considers such an abstract analysis of truth to be of little genuine value. But he concludes from this that James's theory is not to be seen as competing with traditional accounts of truth, since their questions are not identical. According to Thayer, James considers traditional coherence and correspondence theories to be concerned with the formal definition of truth, while James is interested in its pragmatic meaning. Thus, according to Thayer, James considers traditional theories not to be incorrect, but only vague and uninformative.[59] He sees James as intending to amplify and make more concrete the contentions of traditional theories by bringing out the

practical consequences of their definitions and pro-
nouncements. But according to Thayer, James's own
theory is not meant to contradict or compete with traditional theories. It is designed to perform a different
task.

But James was aiming for more than this. While his
remarks are often ambiguous,[60] on balance it seems
clear that he seeks to repudiate the coherence and correspondence theories. Since, according to James, the
concept of truth derives its meaning from the concrete
particulars to which it refers, it follows that any realist
conception of truth—such as in the correspondence
and coherence theories in which truth exists prior to its
concrete instantiations—would have to be considered
meaningless. Thus, in *The Meaning of Truth*, James contends that non-pragmatic conceptions of truth are
meaningless:

> Leave out that whole notion of *satisfactory working* or *lead-
> ing* (which is the essence of my pragmatistic account) and
> call truth a static logical relation, independent even of *pos-
> sible* leadings or satisfactions, and it seems to me you cut all
> ground from under you. . . .

> There is, in short, no *room* for any grade or sort of truth
> outside of the framework of the pragmatic system.[61]

We must conclude, then, that James intends his account of truth to replace traditional theories, and also
that he sees himself as answering the same question
traditional theorists have addressed. Yet it should also
be clear that in his attempt to deal with the question of
truth in the most concrete possible way James approaches the issue from a new direction. The new departure in James's theory is the idea that truth is a
functional category. The truth of a belief depends on
whether it works—whether it passes the tests of satisfactoriness and verifiability in the subject's experience.
Thus James holds that truth cannot be known "save as
that which inclines belief." [62] And he assumes as well
that individuals will be inclined to hold only those beliefs which function adequately. In *Pragmatism* he states

that "the reasons why we call things true is the reason why they *are* true." [63] Thus James interprets the question, "By virtue of what is a given proposition true?," to mean "By virtue of what does the subject justifiably *call* that proposition true?" And this is the central conceptual point in his analysis of truth. The question of the meaning of truth is reduced in James's hands to the question of the criteria by which the subject's beliefs are justified.[64]

We have seen that James bases his analysis of truth upon individual "truths" because he holds the view that truth is exhaustively analyzable in terms of actual or possible experiences. It is this idea that makes James's theory powerful and interesting. But it also results in one of the theory's most serious difficulties. The initial premise of James's theory is that the concept of truth can be meaningful only if it functions as descriptive of human experience. "Truth," for James, is a purely descriptive term—an abstraction from particular truths encountered in experience. It has no meaning apart from its (actual or possible) empirical instantiations. But in taking this position James fails to recognize that the concept of truth is an explanatory and not a descriptive one. While there may possibly be some initial plausibility in the attempt to articulate the meaning of empirical concepts in exclusively experiential terms,[65] this sort of analysis is considerably less plausible in the case of theoretical concepts such as truth. The primary function of the concept of truth is not to *describe* any item or set of items in experience, but rather to provide an *explanation* of why we may justifiably make certain judgments about experiential (and other) phenomena. To say that a belief is true is not, as James would have it, to describe it as being verifiable or satisfactory. Rather, it is to explain why it is verifiable or satisfactory. The explanation lies in the fact that true propositions accurately represent reality—independently of human experience and belief. This notion of truth certainly has its drawbacks, several of which James articulates with great force. Still the essential point to be preserved is that the truth of a judgment *about* experience cannot itself be considered an item *of* experience, however complex.[66]

One of James's reasons for rejecting any transexperiential concept of truth appears to be the concern that if truth were separable from experience, there would be no reliable basis upon which truth could be ascribed. But there seems little reason to consider this a problem. A concept need not itself be descriptive of experience in order to be capable of reliably being ascribed on the basis of experience. To deny this would be to undermine the meaning of any theoretical or explanatory concepts — a position which is clearly unreasonable.

Perhaps the chief cost of failing to recognize the explanatory function of the concept of truth is that it leaves one unable to account for the fact that, in some cases, the most plausible account of the subject's experience is that he has discovered what was already independently true, where such a truth is indeed independent of the experience of *any* individual. For that matter, we have seen that James himself makes reference to such an idea when he describes absolute truth as an ideal set of formulations which do not change with time and which are independent of ever actually being believed. But we have also seen that such a notion goes beyond the limits of James's experientialism.

Thus we must conclude that James's attempt at an exclusively experiential account of truth is incompatible with the requirement that the concept of truth serve an explanatory function. While James can be credited with taking the experiential aspects of truth to their limits in a sophisticated and innovative theory, the theory nevertheless falls short in this important respect.

7. James's Conception of Reality

JAMES'S VIEWS ON THE nature of reality are among the most complex and tangled parts of his philosophy. An examination of his writings on this topic reveals unexpected changes in focus and perspective, and an array of diverse claims that have baffled the commentators. Nowhere is there more disagreement and uncertainty among James scholars than there is with regard to this part of his philosophy. In this chapter we shall consider the various claims James makes about reality—claims that often appear incompatible—for the sake of articulating a coherent point of view.

Part of the problem in understanding James's view comes from the fact that he approaches the question of reality from two quite different perspectives; and with each perspective he is addressing a different problem and is concerned with "reality" in a different sense. One of these perspectives finds its fullest expression in James's pragmatic writings, particularly Chapter 5 of *Pragmatism*, and "Professor Hébert on Pragmatism" in *The Meaning of Truth*; as well as in *The Principles of Psychology*.[1] In these writings James deals with the question of the nature of reality in terms of the reality of ordinary physical objects. Here reality is considered from a "common-sense" point of view. James differentiates this from the scientific or philosophical points of view, for example, according to which physical objects might be construed only as convenient names for collections of atoms, or ideas.[2] When James talks about "reality" in the pragmatic sense of this term, he is referring to common-sense physical objects as they are ordinarily understood. When he deals with the nature of such pragmatic realities, he is concerned with the question of what it is for an object to count as real in an individual's life, given the nature of his experiences and his goals.

The second way in which James approaches the question of reality is from a strictly metaphysical point of view that is best developed in his *Essays in Radical Empiricism*.[3] Toward the end of his life, James felt a desire to move beyond the shorter, more popular lectures he had been writing, in order to devote himself to developing a full metaphysical system. Richard Bernstein, in his introduction to James's *A Pluralistic Universe*, quotes from a letter James wrote to Bergson in 1902, describing his intentions:

> My health is so poor now that work goes on very slowly, but I am going, if I live, to write a general system of metaphysics which in many of its fundamental ideas agrees closely with what you have set forth.[4]

While James never did write a sustained treatise in systematic metaphysics, he nevertheless developed a metaphysical theory in a series of writings gathered together under the title *Essays in Radical Empiricism*. In these essays James inquires into the metaphysically basic reality underlying the common-sense objects of our world. It is here that he defends his view that "experience" is the sole and ultimate reality. As we shall see, James considers these two ways of talking about reality to be complementary parts of a larger vision.

In developing his views on reality James had several aims most prominently in mind. Perhaps his most pressing goal was to repudiate the dualistic view that there is an epistemological and metaphysical gap between the subjective knower, on the one hand, and the objective world to be known, on the other—a gap the bridging of which creates perplexing, if not overwhelming, philosophical problems. Historically, responses to these problems have ranged from, at the one extreme, absolute idealism—which goes so far as to require a universal all-embracing Absolute to provide the only possible bridge between subject and object—and, at the other extreme, scepticism—which accedes to the permanent impossibility of any epistemologically adequate relationship between the subject and the external world. James found both of these responses heroic and unnecessary, and he wanted to show that the problem in response to which such philosophies are built is itself spurious. Thus he set out to demonstrate that there is no epistemological or metaphysical gap between the knower and the known, and hence no need for either constructing bridges or lamenting their absence.

Another goal important to James was to repudiate a second classical philosophical dualism—one that has been perhaps even more firmly entrenched than the first. This is the view that the world of physical objects and the world of values are ontologically distinct. On this dualism, moral and aesthetic values are by their nature subjective and personal, or if they are objective, they are nevertheless non-empirical, and hence occupy a dimension of reality entirely separate from the world of physical fact. James considered such a view narrow-minded and false to our sense of life; for as he saw it, the worth of a thing shows itself as indefatigably and unambiguously as do the rest of its qualities.[5]

Despite the clarity of James's intentions, his views on reality themselves have been opaque in important ways. Examining the commentaries on this topic, we find they run the gamut of possible interpretations. E. C. Moore, for instance, contends that James is a phenomenalist—that, like Berkeley, James holds that physical objects are reducible to sense experiences.[6] A. J. Ayer agrees, if the phenomenalistic thesis is put in its linguistic form. He argues that James holds the position he calls "strong phenomenalism"—the view that all significant statements about physical objects are translatable into statements about actual or possible experiences. Alternatively, he claims that James could have gotten most of what he wanted from a weaker form of

phenomenalism—namely, the view that physical objects are nothing but theoretical constructs which we
use to organize and explain our experiences.[7] Others
whose interpretations of James move in the same
phenomenalistic or idealistic direction as Ayer's and
Moore's include his contemporaries A. O. Lovejoy and
B. H. Bode. According to Lovejoy, James intimates that
if the pragmatist is not a pure Berkeleyan idealist, he
must at least be a panpsychist.[8] And Bode objects to
James on the grounds that his position is inevitably sol-
ipsistic.[9]

There are other scholars, however, who opt for an
opposite point of view and argue that James is realistic
in his metaphysics—that is to say, that for James physical objects exist independently of the knowing subject.
Thus Robert G. Meyers contends that James holds a
version of natural or naive realism—namely, the view
that in perceiving we are directly aware of independently existing objects.[10] Andrew Reck also holds that
James is a realist. He argues that James began as a
naive realist, but that he later abandoned that position
in favor of perspectival realism—namely, the view that
"varying percepts are related to a single object when
they are focused on a common location in space." [11]

Such a divergence of interpretations is indeed surprising. But more perplexing still is the fact that James's
text appears to support them all, as I shall illustrate
with the quotations that follow. At one point, for instance, James concedes that "pragmatism is compatible
with solipsism." [12] Elsewhere, in favor of a phenomenalistic interpretation, we find claims like the following:

> Berkeley's criticism of "matter" was consequently abso-
> lutely pragmatistic. Matter is known as our sensations of
> colour, figure, hardness and the like. They are the cash-
> value of the term. . . . These sensations then are its sole
> meaning.[13]

> Reality, howsoever remote, is always defined as a terminus
> within the general possibilities of experience. . . . [14]

The following passage supports the interpretation of James as opting for a weaker form of phenomenalism:

> The greatest common-sense achievement, after the discovery of one Time and one Space, is probably the concept of permanently existing things. . . . That our perceptions mean *beings* . . . becomes an interpretation so luminous of what happens to us that, once employed, it never gets forgotten. It applies with equal felicity to things and persons, to the objective and to the ejective realm.[15]

On the other side, James appears equally committed to a form of realism:

> As a pragmatist I have . . . carefully posited "reality" *ab initio*, and . . . throughout my whole discussion, I remain an epistemological realist.[16]

> Schiller, Dewey and I are all (I, at *any* rate!) epistemological realists,—the reality known exists independently of the knower's idea, and *as* conceived, if the conception be a true one.[17]

> I am . . . postulating here a standing reality independent of the idea that knows it.[18]

While I do not think it is possible to render consistent all of James's claims about reality, nevertheless his remarks as a whole lose much of their contradictory appearance once we understand that James uses the concept of reality in two different ways. In an important sense objects do exist independently of the subject on James's theory, and this is what has led to his avowals of realism and to realistic interpretations of his philosophy. Of equal importance, however, is the fact that James defines reality in terms of experience, and this has led to idealistic interpretations. How these two views cohere in James's philosophy will become clear as our discussion proceeds.

I

Let us now examine James's pragmatic account of reality, keeping in mind that there is an alternative scheme in his philosophy which we shall consider in turn. In *The Principles of Psychology* James holds that there are "many worlds"—a number of different orders of reality—including the world of science, the world of abstract truths, the supernatural world, the world of commonly accepted prejudices, and others.[19] James holds that each of these kinds of reality is equally legitimate, within its own sphere. From among these worlds, however, James considers the world of physical objects perceived by the senses to be the paramount reality.[20] The reason is that more than any other realities, physical objects affect us most deeply in terms of the fulfillment of our ends. Thus from the pragmatic point of view, they are the most important. When James comes to provide a pragmatic account of reality, then, his focus is on the reality of physical objects—and the question he finds most salient is "What are physical objects 'known-as' in the life of the individual?"

James's account of reality, when seen from the pragmatic point of view, is bipolar. On the one side is the teleological subject with interests, values, and concerns, active in the knowing process; on the other side the flux of his experience. As we have seen in Chapter 2, James pictures the subject as being barraged by continuous sensory input. The rich detail of the flux of experience provides the basis for a vast number of interpretations. The challenge facing the individual is to find his way among the chaotic stream of experience, selecting and arranging them in order to construct a comprehensible world.[21] As a sculptor, beginning with a block of marble, comes to create a statue by cutting away some parts of the stone and highlighting others, on James's view the subject carves specific objects out of the flux of experience. On the basis of his interests and his interest-laden conceptual categories, the individual selectively attends to the complex sensory flux impinging upon him and organizes it in certain ways. The result is "reality-for-him," that is to say, "pragmatic reality." Pragmatic realities, then, are constructed, and the construction proceeds by means of the stream of experience becoming conceptualized, or as James also puts it, "intellectualized." [22] As James describes it, "reality is an accumulation of our own intellectual inventions." [23]

Except in the most extraordinary circumstances, James holds, the subject never perceives experience in its pure, uncategorized form. He makes the point in *Pragmatism*:

> When we talk of reality "independent" of human thinking, then, it seems a thing very hard to find. It reduces to the notion of what is just entering into experience, and yet to be named, or else to some imagined aboriginal presence in experience, before any belief about the presence had arisen, before any human conception had been applied. It is what is absolutely dumb and evanescent, the merely ideal limit of our minds. We may glimpse it, but we never grasp it; what we grasp is always some substitute for it which previous human thinking has peptonized and cooked for our consumption.[24]

This means that it makes no pragmatic sense to speak of "absolute" realities, or realities independent of the subject's constructive act. If what is real is to be understood at all, it must be understood as what is real-for-the-individual.

James contends, then, that pragmatic reality is a creation or construction. The sensible flux tolerates many different interpretations, depending upon the different purposes and interests of whoever is experiencing it. Whatever is there may be experienced differently by each percipient, and for each may be a different object. Let us take a concrete example. While touring San Francisco, as a group of us approaches Fifth and Mission Streets, we each intellectualize the given flux of experience in certain ways, each constituting his own pragmatic reality. Thus, for example, I experience a coin museum, the person on my right, who is a building contractor, experiences a granite edifice, and the person on my left experiences the historic building known as the Old San Francisco Mint. In an important sense, the objects we each perceive are not identical. For each of us constitutes his own particular object out of the flux of experience. James is not to be interpreted here as claiming that there is a single object before us, existing independently of any subject, which is merely interpreted differently by each of us. On the other hand, he does not intend to be understood as denying the existence of real physical objects in the world. Indeed, James's aim is to assert both that real physical objects exist, and that reality is constituted by the subject. He holds that in the pragmatically constructive process, the individual is in direct contact with the real physical objects of the world in which he lives.

This view certainly would be considered paradoxical, if not contradictory, by anyone who presupposed a realist conception of physical objects. For on the realist hypothesis as it is ordinarily understood, it would make no sense to speak of objective physical reality — enduring, material, and mind-independent — as being the result of the subject's constitutive acts. Indeed, presumptions of realism aside, it is difficult to see how James can account for the fact that the world of physical objects as we know it is a shared world, a world in which separate individuals have the same objects in common. While we shall have more to say about this below, let us simply note now that James does not mean to suggest that each person's reality is idiosyncratic, or that reality is determined solely by subjective desire or interest. For James, the latitude permitted in the construction of pragmatic realities is bounded by the nature of experience itself. While the flux of sensation allows for the construction of many different objects, it is not the case that any such construction will be possible:

> There is a push, an urgency, within our very experience, against which we are on the whole powerless, and which drives us in a direction that is the destiny of our belief.[25]

James's analysis of pragmatic reality may be illumi-
nated by the following metaphor. Picture an individual
facing a piece of screening. His aim is to trace a design
beginning from one point on the screen's grid, say the
upper-right-hand corner; and ending at another, say
the lower-left. He need not take the most direct path,
but may take any path he wishes. Thus many designs
are possible. But still his choice is not infinite, for each
design must be in accord with the characteristics of the
grid itself. He cannot go in directions or make patterns
that the grid fails to provide. Some pathway, already
on the grid, is the one he must follow. On James's conception of the relation between the flux of experience
and pragmatic realities, the flux of experience constitutes the screening, the skeleton that we must use in
tracing our designs. First, by acting in some ways
rather than others, we help determine which experiences are accessible to us. Then, from out of the flux
we select which experiences to attend to, i.e., which
paths to follow. And then by investing more importance in some experiences over others, by conceptually
organizing our experiences in groups of our own
devising—in short, by bringing to work our preferences, goals, interests, and emotional investments—we
construct along the determined grids a design that is
most compatible with our purposes and interests. This
design is the world of physical objects, pragmatically
understood.

The world as we know it, then—pragmatic reality—
is a human construction, built upon the principle of
the fulfillment of human interests. Reality-for-the-
individual is determined by those beliefs about reality
which function most satisfactorily in his life. The notion of satisfactorily functioning belief is, of course, one
whose importance we have already observed in James's
philosophy—as the key concept in his theory of truth.
Indeed, pragmatic reality, for James, is nothing other
than the object of pragmatically true beliefs:

Realities in themselves can be there *for* any one . . . only by
being believed; they are believed only by their notions ap-

pearing true; and their notions appear true only because they work satisfactorily.[26]

We have seen in Chapter 4 that the fulfillment of human interests is the criterion determining moral value for James. As truth is a value category, because it embodies the fulfillment of human interests, so also is reality. On James's view the pragmatically constructed world of physical objects is inexpungibly value-laden—pragmatic realities necessarily embody human desires, interests, and ideals. Appealing to Lotze, James articulates his conception of the knower's morally generative role in determining reality:

> Lotze has in several places made a deep suggestion. We naively assume, he says, a relation between reality and our minds which may be just the opposite of the true one. Reality, we naturally think, stands ready-made and complete, and our intellects supervene with the one simple duty of describing it as it is already. But may not our descriptions, Lotze asks, be themselves important additions to reality? And may not previous reality itself be there, far less for the purpose of appearing unaltered in our knowledge, than for the very purpose of stimulating our minds to such additions as shall enhance the universe's total value?[27]

In a letter to Ralph Barton Perry, James is most articulate in describing reality's value-laden character:

> You speak of "*the* world." *The* world is surely the *total* world, including our mental reaction. The world *minus* that is an abstraction, useful for certain purposes, but always envelopable. Pure naturalism is surely envelopable in wider teleological or appreciative determinations.[28]

II

In a lecture in *Pragmatism* that is in some ways extraordinarily modern in tone, James describes how there may be alternative conceptual systems used to characterize any given phenomenon—just as, for example, we may choose to call something either an apple or a collection of molecules. Moreover, James makes the point that the main criterion for choosing among different kinds of descriptions is not whether one is truer than another. Rather, we look to see which description is more appropriate, given the purposes we have in view. The interpretation of our experience in terms of pragmatically functional common-sense objects, which we have just described in the previous section, is only one of several alternatives:

> Science and critical philosophy . . . burst the bounds of common sense. With science *naif* realism ceases: "Secondary" qualities become unreal; primary ones alone remain. With critical philosophy, havoc is made of everything. The common-sense categories one and all cease to represent anything in the way of *being*; they are but sublime tricks of human thought, our ways of escaping bewilderment in the midst of sensation's irremediable flow.[29]

James's theory of radical empiricism is his attempt to analyze the nature of reality on the critical philosophical level of thought. His intention is not to reject the pragmatic realities of common sense, described in ordinary language, but rather to show their ultimate metaphysical basis, and to place them in the context of a metaphysical theory. We shall consider below the extent to which James succeeds in approaching the question of reality from these two different standpoints.

James calls his metaphysical theory "radical empiricism." It is an empiricism in that its leading postulate is that "everything real must be experienceable somewhere, and every kind of being experienced must somewhere be real."[30] It is radical, James maintains, because the relations between things are held to be as real and as much a part of experience as are the things themselves.[31] While an intricate discussion of James's radical empiricism would take us far beyond the scope of this book, nevertheless it will be worthwhile to consider the main outlines of the theory.[32]

The ultimate metaphysical reality, on James's view, is

"pure experience," which he describes as coming in a continuous stream, with each part of it leading to the next, the boundaries of each fusing together: "in the real concrete sensible flux of life experiences compenetrate each other." [33] The flux of experience has a continuously widening periphery. There is always another experience in any set of them, if the flow of experience is allowed to continue. It is a continuous, flowing, ever-expanding reality.[34] While it is always possible, by using concepts, to analyze experience into discrete bits for the sake of practical purposes, it is not to be thought that experience is actually composed of separate units. By using concepts we arrest the stream of experience, take static cuts of it, like a single frame in a moving picture. Conceptual thought does not represent experience as it truly is, for experience is continuous and changing, and concepts are discontinuous and fixed.[35]

Thus James takes issue with those philosophers and philosophical systems which pose the problem of uniting experience into a coherent meaningful whole. For James's view is that such a problem simply does not arise when experience is properly understood. His frequent polemics against the idealists, who require an all-embracing Absolute relator of experiences, as well as those against the associationists, who after dividing experience are left with the question of how to relate what they have separated, stem from his belief in an antecedent unity to all experience which obviates the necessity of connecting its parts.

James calls pure experience a "materia prima." [36] While it is unlike Aristotle's prime matter in that pure experience is not entirely undifferentiated,[37] still the title is deserved. For by itself pure experience constitutes no definite thing or things. As the prior metaphysical basis of things, James contends that it is not anything specific in itself.[38]

James's metaphysical doctrine of pure experience involves an unequivocal repudiation of some of the best-entrenched philosophical dualisms. The distinction between thoughts and things, as well as the associated distinctions between mental and physical, subject and object, knower and known, consciousness and the object of consciousness, are considered by James to be only common-sense or practical distinctions, having no ontological status. Since pure experience is all there is, these terms do not designate metaphysically distinct sorts of entities. They stand only for distinguishable functions within experience itself. Indeed, for James, even personal consciousness is nothing but "the name for a series of experiences run together by certain definite transitions." [39] James explains that any given experience — itself metaphysically neutral — may be taken as physical or taken as mental, depending upon the context of other experiences with which it is associated.[40] Things and thoughts, then, are nothing but sets of experiences related in certain ways.

To illustrate his view that one thing can be taken in two different ways, depending upon its context of associates, James uses the following metaphor. He has us imagine a quantity of artist's paint, and the different contexts in which it can be found. When the paint is in a pot in a paint shop, along with other paints similarly packaged, it counts as something to be bought and sold. When the same paint is spread on a canvas, however, surrounded by other paints, it is an aesthetically functional element in a picture. Similarly, James maintains, the same piece of experience may function as a thought in one context, while in another context it may function as a thing.[41]

To elucidate his view that "thoughts" and "things" are merely functional, contextual distinctions within experience, James asks the reader to focus on a perceptual experience — say, that of the room in which he sits. He claims that in such a case of direct perception, the percipient will be unable to differentiate his perception into consciousness (thought) on the one hand, and the object of consciousness (thing) on the other. James concludes from this that thought and the object of thought are identical, and hence that the percipient must be in direct contact with the room itself.[42] While on a dualistic view of mind and matter such a situation would appear to be most difficult, James's pure experience philosophy provides a ready explanation. For James, the room as a physical object and the room as a mental content are one and the same pure experience, taken in different contexts. To explain how the room as a physical object can be identical with the room as a mental content is as simple as explaining how one identical point can be on two lines. As a single point may occur at the intersection of two lines, and thus be part of them both, a single experience may occur at the intersection of two different trains of associated experiences. Thus in perceptual knowledge the individual's experience of the room occurs at the intersection of two lines: the first line is the set of experiences which constitute his personal biography, the second is the history and future of the house of which the room is a part:

> The presentation, the experience, . . . is the last term of a train of sensations, emotions, decisions, movements, classifications, expectations, etc., ending in the present, and the first term of a series of similar "inner" operations extending into the future, on the reader's part. On the other hand, the very same *that* is the *terminus ad quem* of a lot of previous physical operations, carpentering, papering, furnishing, warming, etc., and the *terminus a quo* of a lot of future ones, in which it will be concerned when undergoing the destiny of a physical room.[43]

III

Having previously examined James's idea of pragmatic reality, and having now outlined his metaphysical notion of reality as pure experience, we may consider the relationship between the two views. James always speaks as though his two approaches to the question of reality were consistent, but he does not specifically address himself to the relation between them. The two views are indeed consistent on many important points, but still their relation is not entirely unproblematic. On a structural level, we find the two views to be isomorphic. From the pragmatic point of view, different common-sense objects can be constructed by subjects relating differently to the flux of experience. From the point of view of radical empiricism, there are of course neither subjects nor objects, but only pure experience. "Subjects" and "objects" are reduced to sets of experiences which can be distinguished within the continuous flux. These distinguishable sets are related in certain ways. For a subject to constitute a common-sense object out of the flux of experience, translated into the language of radical empiricism, is for a given set of experiences (the "subject") to be united with other sets of experiences (the "object") through a specific relation. The relation may be "knowing," "believing," "perceiving," or the like. Thus the two views are compatible in their gross anatomy. We must remember here that relations, too, are pure experiences on James's theory of radical empiricism, and hence his notion of pure experience as constituting all of reality is in no way violated by this scheme.

There is nevertheless considerable tension between these two views of reality. First, it would appear that James cannot reasonably claim in his pragmatic writings that the pragmatically constructed physical objects of our everyday world are real—that physical objects are real exactly as they are experienced—and yet claim in *Essays in Radical Empiricism* that these objects are nothing more than mere functional distinctions. For if physical objects are merely functional distinctions within the sole metaphysically ultimate stuff of pure experience, their reality would seem to be seriously impugned.

This objection may be dealt with by fully articulating what it means to say, as James does, that "reality" is used in different ways on different conceptual levels. Just as one would not call an apple unreal because it is

also a collection of molecules (if one did, there would
be no real apple with which an unreal apple—say a
wax apple—could be contrasted), similarly a physical
object may well be real on the common-sense level,
even if on the metaphysical level it counts not as an
entity but as a function within pure experience. Within
the pragmatically real world of lived experience, physical objects are ultimately real, and cannot be called into
question. That they may be reduced to functions within
pure experience on a metaphysical level does not viti-
ate their full *pragmatic* reality. Thus James's theory of
pure experience does not undermine his pragmatic account.

Yet a serious difficulty remains. If we accept the
existence of pragmatic realities on the basis of James's
principle that reality is what it is known-as, then his
conception of reality as pure experience would seem to
have no place in his philosophy. For as we have seen
pure experience, however paradoxically, is not itself
experienceable. James's analysis of pragmatic reality is
an exemplification of his use of the pragmatic method.
As we have seen in many instances, this is a method by
which James reduces the meaning of metaphysical issues to their respective practical consequences. As such,
it represents a denial of the legitimacy and meaningfulness of speculative metaphysics. Yet in *Essays in Radical Empiricism* James moves beyond the principles of his
pragmatism, into the very sort of metaphysics the
pragmatic method is designed to circumvent. For what
practical or concrete difference can it make if the ultimate constitution of reality is pure experience, rather
than, say, mind and matter? If reality is what it is
known-as, then pure experience cannot be pragmatically meaningful.

Another point of stress between James's two accounts
of reality is found in his conception of the subject of
experiences. We have seen that, in his analysis of
pragmatic reality, James relies heavily on the notion of
a teleological subject actively constituting his world in
accordance with his purposes and interests. In *Essays in*

Radical Empiricism, on the other hand, James denies
that consciousness as an entity, or any subject of experiences, exists. But if the subject itself is reduced to a
stream of experiences, it appears impossible to account
for the teleological qualities of mind which play such a
central role in James's pragmatic view.

While this objection certainly illuminates the radically different emphases and priorities in each of
James's theories of reality, it is not clear that it points to
any actual contradictions in his philosophy. For James
would claim that there is no meaning to the concept of
a teleological subject or agent over and above what can
be specified as teleological activities. Teleological activity, in turn, designates nothing other than a certain
functional arrangement of experiences. Teleological
activities, for James, are simply organized sets of experiences, including experiences of interest, desire, striving, resistance, fulfillment of goal, and the like.[44] Thus,
James would hold that the teleological subject of his
pragmatic writings is fully accounted for in terms of his
radical empiricism. Whether it is possible to provide a
reductive analysis of teleological activities in this way is
a question still at issue among philosophers. We may at
least note, however, that James was cognizant of the
need to provide such an analysis, and that he at-
tempted to do so.

Having considered both James's metaphysical and
pragmatic approaches to the question of reality, we can
now see how such a wide range of contradictory interpretations of his view could have been proposed. On
the one hand, commentators who have called James a
realist are correct in recognizing that on his view of
perceptual knowledge, the subject is in direct contact
with the real, common-sense physical objects of the
world. Nevertheless, James is not a realist, if this requires that the subject's real world is external to his experience of it, or independent of all experience. For as
we have seen, James holds that while the object known
is a real physical object, it is nevertheless constructed by
the knower and reducible to experience.

On the other hand, commentators who have considered James to be an idealist are correct in recognizing that, for him, reality is ultimately reducible to experience. They are incorrect, however, to treat "experience" as a subjective or mentalistic notion in his philosophy. For the point of James's metaphysical system, as we have seen, is to show that the subject/object distinction is valid only as a functional distinction *within* experience—experience itself being neither subjective nor objective, but the ground of both.

On the basis of the foregoing considerations we must conclude that the usual dichotomy between realism and idealism is simply inapplicable to James's philosophy. Rather, the most appropriate designation for his view as it applies to physical objects is that it is a protophenomenology: common-sense objects as constituted by the subject within lived experience are the ultimately real physical objects of our world. There is a developing literature on the relation between James and phenomenology.[45] Some commentators find the relation a close one, while others are more circumspect. It is apparent to all, however, that there are numerous similarities between the philosophies of James and his contemporary Husserl, and without attempting to specify the magnitude of it here, it is clear that Husserl owes a debt to James.[46]

The results are more ambiguous when we try to classify James's theory of reality on the deepest metaphysical level, for James himself is ambiguous about the ultimate status of experience in his philosophy. While he holds "pure experience" to be neutral between subject and object, mind and matter, he does not always treat it in this way. Frequently, he uses the notion of experience mentalistically. For instance, he describes pure experience as "sensation,"[47] and experience as "just what appears,"[48] and as "the instant field of the present."[49] Elsewhere, however, James appears to leave it as an open question whether experience could exist if there were no minds at all.[50] Clearly, some questions in James's metaphysics remain unresolved.

Finally, let us turn to one of the most serious difficulties confronting James's view. We have seen that James considers common-sense physical objects to be the product of a pragmatic construction. On this position realities may differ, depending upon personal interpretations of experience. But the problem here is that such a constructionalist view of reality, whatever its novelty or interest, seems to founder irretrievably upon the question of the objective world. For it would seem that on this position, each person would reflect experience from his own idiosyncratic point of view, and constitute his own private world of personal objects. But James tries to show that in fact such a situation does not occur. We have enough in common with one another, he claims, to share in the reality of a common world. In the first place, our experiences themselves are roughly similar. In the second place, we share a common physical nature, a common human condition, and in a general way, common interests and common conceptual categories for interpreting experience. Hence the worlds we constitute are by and large the same.

This is not an adequate answer to the objection, however, for objectivity requires more than the simultaneous constitution, by different minds, of numerically different even if qualitatively identical worlds.[51] It requires a single world, held in common by us all. James does not fail to recognize this point, and he responds by arguing that the determination of whether we share a common world cannot itself be established by reference to anything but that world as it is experienced. Any qualities of a common world which are not capable of being manifested in experience pragmatically count as nothing for us. We perceive a common world of common objects, James claims, because your object and mine function as the same object, for all relevant purposes, in the context of experience and action. He argues as follows:

> For instance, your hand lays hold of one end of a rope and my hand lays hold of the other end. We pull against

each other. Can our two hands be mutual objects in this experience, and the rope not be mutual also? What is true of the rope is true of any other percept. Your objects are over and over again the same as mine. If I ask you *where* some object of yours is, our old Memorial Hall, for example, you point to *my* Memorial Hall with *your* hand which *I* see. If you alter an object in your world, put out a candle, for example, when I am present, *my* candle *ipso facto* goes out. It is only as altering my objects that I guess you to exist. If your objects do not coalesce with my objects, if they be not identically where mine are, they must be proved to be positively somewhere else. But no other location can be assigned for them, so their place must be what it seems to be, the same.

Practically, then, our minds meet in a world of objects which they share in common, which would still be there, if one or several of the minds were destroyed.[52]

While not every characteristic of my pragmatic objects will be identical with yours—the object before us may be for me a place to swim, and for you a place to sail a boat—nevertheless, James holds that even in this case both of our objects meet the minimum condition of sharing a common location in space. Moreover, James holds that this, conjoined with the fact that we may influence one another's objects in predictable and law-like ways, constitutes all there is, pragmatically, to the idea of a common world.

But here I think the difficulties of James's reductionistic position are most apparent. The problem is similar to the one we have encountered in his theory of truth. James argues that we cannot meaningfully ask for more than descriptions of facts as they occur. He thinks that it makes no sense to ask for an explanation, beyond experience, for the fact that when you put out your candle, my candle goes out. But this, I think, is incorrect. The question that may legitimately concern us is not whether we can infer, for pragmatic purposes, that your candle and mine are in the same place, but rather whether the candle exists externally to both of us. This requirement of an explanation, while it adds nothing descriptive about the world as we know it, nevertheless is not otiose. For the hypothesis of externally existing objects explains, better than any alternative hypothesis, why our experiences turn out the way they do. We must conclude, then, that while there is very considerable interest, originality, and power in James's theory, his radical empiricism lacks a way of adequately explaining the commonality of our experiences, and hence falters on the problem of objectivity.

8. Summary and Conclusions

THROUGHOUT THIS BOOK WE have examined James's theories, following the outline of his system articulated in Chapter 1. In concluding this study, it will be useful to return to a broad picture of James's system as a whole, taking special note of its motivating doctrines, its implications, and its value.

To review our major conclusions, we have found that in the development of his views, James never forsakes two fundamental commitments which function to unify his system and render it coherent. The first of these is his commitment to the principle of experience — namely, the view that all philosophical issues are properly understood only by reference to their experiential implications and effects. James has a broad sense of what is to count as acceptable under this principle. Though it is not his intention to restrict philosophical inquiry by binding it within narrow sensory limits, he does intend to restrain it from excesses of arid abstraction. Philosophical ideas should be tested by the principle of experience, James maintains, because any idea that does not issue in concrete consequences for human life is otiose. As such, it can only constrain and deflect our energies and interests. The motivation behind James's principle of experience is unquestionably moral in character. Philosophy as a human activity should be used for the furtherance of human ends, and without experiential consequences it can have no worthwhile issue.

Secondly, James is committed to a conception of

human nature which views individuals as motivated toward the fulfillment of a wide range of purposes and interests. Emphasizing the willful and emotional well-springs of thought, James views the goals of the subject as determining the very nature of his concepts and beliefs. Rather than being static essences, quarantined from the interests and concerns of the whole person, ideas are rooted deeply in the individual's own personal and conative stance toward the world. One salutary effect of James's doctrine is the fact that it clarifies and emphasizes the fuller significance of thought. As ideas derive from interests and purposes, they must also answer to them. James emphasizes that intellectual activities have important implications for how we live our lives—affecting what we shall do, what we shall become, what sorts of attitudes we shall have, and even how we shall interpret and change the world. Thus, the kinds of things we think about, the directions to which we turn our philosophical attention, are rife with moral significance. When seen in this way, James, far more fully than many of his protagonists, shows respect for the power and importance of intellectual activities. He rejects only those that are isolated and without larger point.

We have seen how James's commitment to the fundamental principles of his pragmatism informs his system at every point. It is on the basis of the morally relevant, practical function of thought that James develops his theory of meaning. He delineates the sorts of philosophical discussions and claims that are to count as meaningful, and specifies criteria for the determination of their meaning. The hallmark of his analysis lies in his insistence that, for a philosophical contention to be meaningful, it must not lose contact with the concrete problematic which generated it, or with the possibility of leading to concrete future consequences for thought, feeling, and conduct. James works this out in his view that, to be meaningful, a philosophical contention must both entail that certain consequences will occur and generate consequences in the life of the person who holds it.

One result of this approach is that at certain points James's theory appears ambiguous in its focus and aim. On the one hand, there are instances where James seems to be giving a purely empirical account relating the different functions beliefs have in human life, and the ways in which they are important. On the other hand, there are instances where James seems concerned to provide an analysis of the cognitive meaning of the proposition believed, in the sense of its abstract intelligible purport. Moreover, James seems to draw no clear distinction between these two approaches to the question. A closer examination of James's theory, however, shows that this is not as much a problem as it may first appear. For the point of his theory is to place the question of meaning on a new footing. In what may best be called a theory of pragmatic meaning, James rejects the distinction between meaning and empirical function. He argues for a new and enriched notion of meaning, wherein the empirical functions of an idea or belief actually constitute its meaning, in any sense of "meaning" which has philosophical value.

Turning to James's ethical theory, the view that "the essence of good is the satisfaction of demand," we note once again his use of the principle of experience. James holds that moral principles cannot exist a priori or lie beyond experience in any way whatever. His ethical naturalism is based on his conception of human beings as positors of ends, and the only plausible repository of ethical value, he finds, is thus in the fulfillment of those ends—in the form of interests, desires, goals, and ideals.

James's ethical theory begins from the subjective starting point of the single individual. He imagines a "moral solitude"—a world with a single person having demands. From this he aims to show that consciousness is required if moral concepts are to have any meaning; indeed that moral value is subjectively generated by the individual. It is from this model that James derives the idea that the satisfaction of demand is the basis of moral value. He then goes on to develop a scheme for an objective morality, given the fact that we exist not in solitude, subjectively generating values relevant only to ourselves, but as a community of persons with complex and multiple demands whose inevitable conflicts must be adjudicated in an unbiased way.

James's analysis of moral concepts exclusively in terms of human experience has the advantage that moral value is embodied in the human situation and accessible to being known. Moreover, James is correct in placing human desires, needs, and aims in a central position in his theory. To be adequate an ethical theory must reflect the psychological conditions under which we act and through which we interpret our situations, and if it does not give due consideration to these motivational factors so central to the way we lead our lives, it will give a false account of the meaning of moral concepts. Nevertheless there are problems with James's theory, fundamental problems in identifying moral value with the satisfaction of demand. For it seems clear that there exist states of affairs which are valuable, even if they are not perceived to be so, even if they satisfy no demands. Moreover, there exist states of affairs in which demands are fully satisfied, but which nevertheless are bad.

It is worth noting, however, that James himself did not feel bound by the satisfaction-of-demand model. In his many discussions of various ethical issues, he expresses with great force and commitment several substantive ethical judgments that go well beyond it—most notably the view that moral strenuousness and rigorous commitment to ideals are among the highest goods.

James's views on the justification of belief also show the influence of his teleological conception of mind. While his work on the issue of the will to believe is well known, it is also correspondingly less well understood. His major accomplishment has been to move beyond the traditional assumption that there is only one criterion according to which a belief is justified—namely, the extent to which it is supported by adequate evidence. James argues that in some cases the ultimate attainment of adequate evidence requires belief prior to such evidence. His most influential point, however, concerns not the evidence for a belief, but rather the phenomenon of believing itself. James recognizes that in some cases a person's belief may well lead to important consequences in his life—in terms of his perceptions, attitudes, feelings, commitments, capabilities, and actions. On this ground he reaches the striking conclusion that the beneficial moral or prudential consequences which follow from holding a belief may justify holding that belief, even if it is not supported by adequate evidence. James bases his case on the idea that believing is not merely an abstract intellectual exercise, and therefore that its assessment should not be restricted to the single criterion of evidential warrant. Believing, like acting, hoping, and planning, is one of the many modes in which we enact our lives as teleologically oriented individuals. James's point is that any philosophy is naive and impoverished which posits criteria of justification of belief without recognizing this more full and active conception of the role of belief in a person's life. James makes a powerful case for this position, and it must be concluded that the academic critics who have rejected as intellectually disreputable the possibility of pragmatically justifying belief have not given sufficient weight to the diverse functions which beliefs may have.

James does recognize, of course, that there are many cases in which the only way a belief may be justified is on the basis of adequate evidence. But since he also supports a pragmatic justification, he is left with the problem of determining which criterion of justification, the pragmatic or the evidential, should prevail in cases of conflict. While James does not deal with this problem, it is by no means clear that an abstract decision-procedure in advance of actual cases would be reasonable or even possible. Nevertheless it would have been appropriate, in order to prevent the legitimation of irrationally held beliefs, for James to provide somewhat more specific guidelines than he did. We may conclude, then, that while the application of James's pragmatic criterion for the justification of belief could be problematic in some cases, there is no doubt that this criterion is often appropriate and valuable, and that James's defense of it is a successful and important contribution to epistemology and the ethics of belief.

James's theory of truth is the pinnacle of his philosophical system. In this theory James utilizes all the mechanisms he has previously developed to generate a sophisticated and delicately balanced product of pragmatic philosophy. His principle of experience plays a major role in the theory. By reducing truth to actual or possible judgments of truth, James delineates the meaning of truth in exclusively experiential terms. His view of the teleological character of mind also has a central place in his theory of truth. On the basis of his view that the function of belief is to answer interests, James contends that a belief is true to the extent that it is "satisfactory"—to the extent that it enables the believer most inclusively to fulfill his purposes and answer his interests. An important implication of this is that truth is a category of moral value for James. As truth involves the satisfaction of certain sorts of demand, it is, in James's language, "one species of good."

James's theory provides a direct challenge to the historically dominant position that, insofar as an individual's beliefs are dictated by or designed to meet his preferences and goals, they are likely to be less objective and hence less true. But in spite of appearances, on this level of his theory James is not caught in a pernicious subjectivism. This becomes clear when his second requirement of truth is recognized—that true beliefs must be "verifiable." By this James means that a belief cannot count as true unless it is continually confirmed, or at least not disconfirmed, in the subject's experience. Hence there is no latitude in James's theory for beliefs to be true if they are incompatible with experiential conditions, conditions that are not malleable to the subject's personal aims.

James's approach to truth is interesting and unusual in that he attempts to develop an idea of objective truth starting from a subjective standpoint. The structure of his program parallels that of his ethics, where James begins from a subjective "moral solitude" and describes the development of an increasingly objective ethical system. In the theory of truth, James begins from the particular experiences and interests of a single individual at a particular time and gradually arrives at a conception of truth that incorporates the experiences and interests of an increasing number of persons over an increasing period of time. For James, the ideal endpoint of this process is objective, absolute truth. This idea constitutes the critical terminus of James's theory, but it is also the point at which he meets his greatest difficulties.

James thinks about absolute truth on several different levels, searching for an account that will be adequate to all his requirements. On one level he defines absolute truth fully within the context of human experience, where it denotes the ultimate human agreement. But James seems to realize that this notion of absolute truth, depending as it does on actual human opinion, cannot account for the objectivity required of truth. He moves to a deeper analysis, where he conceives of absolute truth as independent of human experience and belief. But this carries its own problems. While a realist conception of truth such as this is indeed required to preserve objectivity, for James to wrest the notion of truth from its concrete workings is to make a significant departure from the rest of his philosophy. To posit absolute truth in this sense is to violate his own principle of experience.

Turning to James's theory of reality, we find that it does not lend itself to easy summary. In fact, we are dealing with two theories. Yet even in this area of his philosophy we find the teleology of mind and the principle of experience operating as pivotal conceptions.

One theory of reality carries James's principle of experience to its uttermost. In his pragmatic writings James takes "experience" merely as providing a test of philosophically legitimate discourse. But in his doctrine of radical empiricism, experience is elevated to the status of the ultimate metaphysical reality. "Pure experience" is all there is. James argues that this basic reality is a continuous, constantly changing, flowing experiential flux. It exists previous to, and provides the ground of, the dualistic distinctions between subject and object, mental and physical, fact and value. These are merely functional distinctions made within the context of pure experience, and have no ultimate metaphysical status themselves.

James also has a theory of reality which deals with the objects of our common-sense world—these are "pragmatic realities." While these common-sense objects are more significant than pure experience from a practical point of view, they are not metaphysically basic. Indeed, they are created by the subject's interaction with pure experience. The physical objects which make up the world in which we live are value-laden constructions generated by the individual as he approaches the flux of experience and interprets it in the light of his own conative functions.

James's metaphysical theory of pure experience provides the theoretical background for his account of pragmatic realities. "Physical objects"—that is to say, the realities of common sense—as well as the subject of experience, are ultimately reducible to pure experience. James takes the theories to be two different ways of describing the same phenomena, and over-all he succeeds in drawing together both theories as part of a single coherent philosophical picture.

Whether James's view is otherwise successful remains open to question, however. One major difficulty in his position lies in his contention that physical objects are nothing over and above the experiential constructions of the individual. For, as I have argued, personally constructed "objects" of multiple individuals cannot substitute for a common objective world.

While I have supported a realist position on truth and reality, in contrast to James, this, of course, is not to suggest that debate is closed on these issues. Indeed, there is important work being done today in epistemology, ontology, and the philosophy of science, which attempts to justify pragmatic and anti-realist points of view. Indeed, many aspects of the current proposals provide evidence of a renascence and furtherance in modern terms of central points in James's philosophy.[1]

One of the most important insights James wished to convey was that it is fruitless to ask about the meaning or value of any phenomenon outside the context of its use in the fulfillment of human ends. This is particularly true when it comes to the assessment of a philosophy itself. As we come to a final assessment of James's philosophy, it will help to be clear about the several kinds of functions philosophy reasonably may be expected to fulfill. On the most traditional conception, the function of philosophy is to arrive at or at least attempt to arrive at the most fundamental objective truths. James's philosophy clearly has a place under this schema, for questions about the nature of reality, the foundation of moral value, the meaning of truth, and the like, constitute the central themes of his pragmatism. Throughout the course of this study we have assessed James's doctrines in detail, and have arrived at conclusions about the extent to which they succeed with regard to their truth.

Success, however, is not to be measured by any single criterion—even the criterion of truth. Philosophy preeminently is, or ought to be, an activity which exercises and elevates the intellect, and which is edifying and inspiriting. From this point of view, the pertinent factors for the assessment of a philosophy become considerations such as the clarity, power, and elegance of the philosopher's arguments; the profundity, subtlety, and originality of his viewpoint; the coherence of his system; the authenticity of his approach; and the consequential intellectual, moral, and personal benefits that come from a serious consideration of his views.

This study has illustrated, I hope, the considerable success of James's philosophy when measured by these criteria. His pragmatism is a sophisticated and coherent system inspired by his commitment to treat philosophy as a serious enterprise, dealing with real problems — problems important to human beings and capable of real solution. James took the philosophical enterprise so seriously because he realized that along with meeting standards of intellectual adequacy and conceptual rigor, a philosophy should provide us with mechanisms for interpreting our experience which are informative, useful, and conducive to the fulfillment of our highest possibilities.

Increasing numbers of philosophers today are drawn to James's philosophy, not only because he is the most vital representative of America's richest philosophical movement, but more importantly because he provides an imaginative and fruitful approach to many philosophical problems and their solutions. James's scope is uncommonly broad. He addresses virtually all of the important issues in philosophy, and he wrote renowned and classical works in psychology and religion as well. To all of the issues he addresses James brings a degree of originality and provocativeness unrivaled in the literature. These attributes, along with the lively eloquence of his style, give his philosophy extraordinary impact. The reader of William James cannot stand outside the inquiry — instead he is drawn into a vivid and subtle dialogue with a man of sensitivity, wisdom, and a profound sense of what is important.

Abbreviations

THE FOLLOWING ABBREVIATIONS are used in the notes for works by William James:

DD   "The Dilemma of Determinism," in *The Will to Believe, The Works of William James*, ed. Frederick H. Burkhardt, Fredson Bowers, and Ignas K. Skrupskelis (Cambridge: Harvard University Press, 1979).

ERE   *Essays in Radical Empiricism, The Works of William James*, ed. Fredson Bowers and Ignas K. Skrupskelis (Cambridge: Harvard University Press, 1976).

LWL   "Is Life Worth Living?," in *The Will to Believe*.

MP   "The Moral Philosopher and the Moral Life," in *The Will to Believe*.

MT   *The Meaning of Truth, The Works of William James*, ed. Fredson Bowers and Ignas K. Skrupskelis (Cambridge: Harvard University Press, 1975).

P   *Pragmatism, The Works of William James*, ed. Fredson Bowers and Ignas K. Skrupskelis (Cambridge: Harvard University Press, 1975).

PP   *The Principles of Psychology*, 2 vols. (New York: Dover Publications, 1950).

PU   *A Pluralistic Universe, The Works of William James*, ed. Fredson Bowers and Ignas K. Skrupskelis (Cambridge: Harvard University Press, 1977).

153

RAAT   "Reflex Action and Theism," in *The Will to Believe.*

SPP   *Some Problems of Philosophy, The Works of William James*, ed. Frederick H. Burkhardt, Fredson Bowers, and Ignas K. Skrupskelis (Cambridge: Harvard University Press, 1979).

SR   "The Sentiment of Rationality," in *The Will to Believe.*

TT   *Talks to Teachers on Psychology and to Students on Some of Life's Ideals* (New York: Dover Publications, 1962).

VRE   *The Varieties of Religious Experience* (New York: Mentor Books, 1958).

WB   "The Will to Believe," in *The Will to Believe.*

Notes

1. James's Pragmatism as a Systematic World-View

1. *Phaedrus*, 246 a, 253 d ff.
2. David Hume, *A Treatise of Human Nature*, bk. 2, sec. 3.
3. *RAAT*, pp. 94–95. James's italics. Throughout this book italics in quotations are in the original unless otherwise specified. See *PP*, 1:8; "Remarks on Spencer's Definition of Mind as Correspondence," in *Essays in Philosophy, The Works of William James*, ed. Frederick Burkhardt, Fredson Bowers, and Ignas K. Skrupskelis (Cambridge: Harvard University Press, 1978), pp. 18, 19–20; *PU*, p. 111.
4. *P*, p. 30.
5. *P*, p. 40.
6. *PU*, p. 149.
7. See *MT*, pp. 68–69; *ERE*, p. 36.
8. "Philosophical Conceptions and Practical Results," in *P*, p. 265.
9. See, for example, *P*, p. 28; "Philosophical Conceptions," in *P*, p. 259; *Essays in Philosophy*, p. 94; *ERE*, p. 81.
10. *P*, p. 32.
11. *P*, pp. 79, 124.
12. *P*, p. 37. Thus, for example, when James is thinking about pragmatism as being merely methodological, he distinguishes his own view from the "humanism" of F. C. S. Schiller, maintaining that while Schiller is committed to a particular view of the nature of truth, he is not. Elsewhere James is emphatic that Schiller's view and his own are identical. See *MT*, pp. 38, 132; Ralph Barton Perry, *The Thought and Character of William James* (Boston: Little, Brown, 1935), 2:487–488.

13. *P*, p. 28.

14. *RAAT*, p. 111.

15. "Philosophical Conceptions," in *P*, p. 265.

16. *P*, p. 97.

17. This is particularly interesting in light of the fact that Peirce, in labeling his philosophy "pragmatism," meant to emphasize the purposive nature of thought. See *The Collected Papers of Charles Sanders Peirce*, Vols. I-VI, ed. Charles Hartshorne and Paul Weiss; VII-VIII, ed. Arthur W. Burks (Cambridge: Harvard University Press, 1931–58), 5.412. (These numbers indicate volume and paragraph: vol. 5, paragraph 412.). While James claims Peirce as the originator of pragmatism, he nevertheless defines his own pragmatism in terms of its emphasis on action, as we have seen. In fact, since purpose plays the central role in James's philosophy, he is far closer to Peirce than he may have recognized when it came to making formal statements of his position.

18. See "Philosophical Conceptions," in *P*, p. 259; *PU*, p. 111.

19. *P*, p. 62.

20. *Utilitarianism*, chap. 4.

2. The Teleology of Mind

1. See *MP*, passim.

2. See *PP*, 1:288; 2:558–559.

3. It is worth noting that, on this description, experience is seen as a subjective stream of sensations, and the subject is differentiated from the external world. James adopts this description as appropriate as long as it is understood as being given from a common-sense or naturalistic point of view. As we shall see in chap. 7, from a metaphysical point of view James denies any dualism between consciousness and the items of consciousness, or between the stream of experience and the external world.

4. *PP*, 1:284 ff.; *RAAT*, pp. 95–96; *P*, pp. 118–119.

5. *RAAT*, p. 95.

6. *PP*, 1:285; see *P*, p. 122.

7. *PP*, 1:285–286.

8. *PP*, 1:285.

9. This assumes that the circle representing the round penny is drawn inside the ellipse representing the elliptical penny. If the ellipse were drawn inside the circle, then we would have the situation—equally inexplicable—of some non-existent points reflecting light.

10. *PP*, 1:289.

11. See *P*, pp. 85, 89, 92, 94.

12. *PP*, 2: chap. 28; see also *MT*, pp. 42–43.

13. In his theory of radical empiricism, James finds that these categories merely reflect relations which are given in the stream of pure experience.

14. *P*, p. 97.

15. *MT*, p. 80; see *TT*, pp. 11–14.

16. *PP*, 2:283.

17. *RAAT*, p. 92; my emphasis.

18. See *PP*, 2:525–528; *TT*, pp. 13, 84–86.

19. *TT*, p. 13.

20. *TT*, p. 14.

21. *TT*, p. 14.

22. *TT*, pp. 83–84.

23. Whether James also holds, as part of this model, that such physiological or neurological changes themselves establish in the individual a disposition to act, he does not really make clear; though with regard to neurological changes, there is some reason to think he intends this.

24. For other passages embodying this conflation, see *PP*, 1:5; 2:527–528.

25. See *RAAT*, p. 103; *MT*, pp. 41, 50–51.

26. See chap. 7 below.

27. See "Remarks on Spencer," *Essays in Philosophy*, pp. 20–22.

3. The Concept of Pragmatic Meaning

1. *P*, chaps. 5, 7, passim; *RAAT*, pp. 91–92, 94–95, 117–120; *SR*, p. 72. *TT*, pp. 13–14; "Remarks on Spencer," in *Essays in Philosophy*, passim; *SPP*, pp. 36, 39; *MT*, pp. 42–43.

2. See H. S. Thayer, *Meaning and Action* (Indianapolis, Ind.: Bobbs-Merrill, 1973), p. 88.

3. A. O. Lovejoy, "The Thirteen Pragmatisms," in *The Thirteen Pragmatisms and Other Essays* (Baltimore, Md.: Johns Hopkins University Press, 1963), pp. 3–10.

4. *Ibid.*, p. 3.

5. *Ibid.*, pp. 6–10.

6. See, for example, Paul Henle, "Introduction on William James," in *Classic American Philosophers*, ed. Max H. Fisch (New York: Appleton-Century-Crofts, 1951), pp. 115–127. Robert G. Meyers, "Meaning and Metaphysics in James," *Philosophy and Phenomenological Research*, 31, no. 3 (March 1971): 369–380.

7. *P*, pp. 53–56.

8. For further discussion of how metaphysical predictions are included under James's predictive import condition, see Meyers, "Meaning and Metaphysics in James."

9. Lovejoy, "The Thirteen Pragmatisms," p. 9; *P*, p. 40.

10. *P*, p. 40; my emphasis.

11. *P*, p. 41; my emphasis.

12. *P*, p. 59.

13. *P*, p. 59.

14. "Philosophical Conceptions," in *P*, p. 264.

15. "What Pragmatism Means by Practical," in *Essays in Experimental Logic* (New York: Dover Publications, n.d.), p. 313.

16. For a fuller discussion of these theories, see for example William P. Alston, *Philosophy of Language* (Englewood Cliffs, N.J.: Prentice-Hall, 1964), chap. 1.

17. *MT*, p. 31n; "Philosophical Conceptions," in *P*, pp. 258–259; *P*, pp. 28–29; *VRE*, pp. 338–339. See Charles S. Peirce, "How to Make Our Ideas Clear," *Collected Papers*, 5.402.

18. *SPP*, p. 37. See *MT*, p. 37.

19. *P*, p. 29.

20. *P*, p. 52.

21. "Philosophical Conceptions," in *P*, p. 260. James later, in *The Meaning of Truth* (p. 103n), changes his mind about this example, and holds that the debate would in fact be meaningful because it would have some pragmatic value. This does not affect his point that if the debate were "purely intellectual" it would be pragmatically meaningless.

22. *VRE*, p. 339.

23. *VRE*, p. 340.

24. "Philosophical Conceptions," in *P*, pp. 268–269.

25. *SPP*, pp. 36–38.

26. Ludwig Wittgenstein, *Philosophical Investigations*, trans. G. E. M. Anscombe (New York: Macmillan, 1953). It should be noted, however, that in describing the use of ideas James was articulating pragmatic meaning as distinct from cognitive meaning. Wittgenstein's intention, on the other hand, was to focus on the use of words and expressions in order to articulate their cognitive meanings.

4. Moral Value

1. "The Moral Philosopher" was published in 1891. "Philosophical Conceptions" was published in 1898.

2. James considers a third major question in the essay as well; it is one which is irrelevant to our concerns here: the psychological genesis of value judgments.

3. *MP*, p. 145.

4. *MP*, p. 145.

5. *MP*, pp. 145–146.

6. *MP*, p. 153.

7. To get this idea across, James often relies on reference to the individual's feelings. See, for instance, his claims that moral qualities can exist only in a "mind which *feels* them" (*MP*, p. 145; my emphasis); "the only possible reason there can be why any phenomenon ought to exist is that such a phenomenon actually is desired" (*MP*, p. 149); and his description of "good," "bad," and "obligation" as "objects of feeling and desire" (*MP*, p. 150).

8. Since, for James, demands are the determinants of moral value, the following passages place demands as a species of judgment. First, in describing a world with only one sentient being:

Outside of [the thinker's] opinion things have no moral character at all [*MP*, p. 146].

Again, in describing a world in which there live two persons who ignore one another:

> The same object is good or bad there, according as you measure it by the view which this one or that one of the thinkers takes. Nor can you find any possible ground in such a world for saying that one thinker's opinion is more correct than the other's, or that either has the truer moral sense [*MP*, p. 146].

In some passages, James appears to use both his first and second senses of "demand" at the same time. In describing the moral solitude, he claims:

> So far as [the individual thinker] feels anything to be good, he *makes* it good. It *is* good, for him [*MP*, p. 146].

The notion of someone feeling something to be good has a curious dual quality about it. James seems to want to capture the ideas both that the object "feels good" to the person— that is to say, that it satisfies the person's desires—and also that the person "feels that," in the sense of "thinks that," the object is good.

9. See *MP*, p. 150, where all three senses of demand are used at once. For a related notion, see James's definition of an ideal, *TT*, p. 142.

10. *MP*, p. 153.

11. *MP*, p. 149.

12. *MP*, p. 147.

13. *MP*, p. 150; see *MP*, p. 145.

14. *MP*, p. 147.

15. Note that James himself makes this same point in *TT*, p. 142.

16. *The Principles of Human Knowledge*, ed. G. J. Warnock (New York: Meridian Books, 1963), pt. 1, sec. 23, pp. 75–76.

17. See *MP*, pp. 159–162; *SR*, pp. 84–89; *DD*, pp. 129–135.

18. *DD*, p. 131.

19. *PP*, 1:315–316.

20. "The Moral Equivalent of War," passim, in *Memories and Studies* (New York: Longmans, Green, 1917).

21. *MP*, p. 153.

22. See *VRE*, pp. 280–282.

23. See *MP*, p. 153.

24. *SR*, p. 87.

25. *DD*, p. 131.

26. *LWL*, p. 45.

27. "What Makes a Life Significant?," in *TT*, p. 133. See also *PP*, 2:578–579.

28. See *P*, pp. 139–140. See also *SR*, p. 71: "We demand in [the universe] a character for which our emotions and active propensities shall be a match." See also *SR*, p. 74, *RAAT*, passim.

29. See *MP*, p. 160.

30. *MP*, p. 161.

31. *MP*, p. 161.

32. *MP*, p. 161.

33. *MP*, p. 161. See also p. 152.

34. *MP*, p. 160.

35. *MP*, p. 153.

36. *MP*, p. 153.

37. *MP*, p. 153.

38. *MP*, p. 155. See also Perry, *Thought and Character*, 2:265; *MP*, pp. 157, 158.

39. Thus, I do not think that John K. Roth is correct when he interprets James's criterion of the satisfaction of demand as being purely quantitative in nature (*Freedom and the Moral Life* [Philadelphia: Westminster Press, 1969], pp. 67–69). James's notion of the inclusiveness of the fulfillment of demands—demands which are multi-dimensional in character—inevitably brings with it some qualitative distinctions between alternative moral choices. Thus, for example, James recommends that in making moral decisions we reject those goods which are not "organizable." By this he means that we should recognize no value in demands which, if fulfilled, would preclude a reasonably balanced fulfillment of all the other demands at hand. (See Perry, *Thought and Character*, 2:254–265.) This is a qualitative criterion. While Roth recognizes James's notion of inclusiveness in the satisfaction of demand, he nevertheless seems to think that this does not bring qualitative considerations into James's theory.

40. *MP*, p. 158.

41. I should imagine he considered the mechanism for

solving an individual's personal moral problems to follow the same pattern, on a smaller scale, as the one we have delineated: consider whoever will be affected by the decision and come to the solution that most inclusively satisfies their demands.

42. *MP*, p. 158.

43. *MP*, p. 156.

44. *MP*, p. 157.

5. Rationality and the Will to Believe

1. See *SR*, pp. 76, 79; *SPP*, p. 111; Perry, *Thought and Character*, 2:211.

2. See "Preface," in *The Will to Believe*.

3. *RAAT*, pp. 104–105.

4. Perry, *Thought and Character*, 2:246.

5. *The Will to Believe*, p. 7.

6. Such a view of justification has been challenged, albeit on grounds other than James's, in recent discussions of foundationalist conceptions of knowledge. See for instance Keith Lehrer, *Knowledge* (Oxford: Clarendon Press, 1974); Frederick L. Will, *Induction and Justification* (Ithaca, N.Y.: Cornell University Press, 1974).

7. John Locke, *An Essay Concerning Human Understanding*, 4th ed., bk. 4, chap. 19 ("Of Enthusiasm"), sec. 1; Descartes, *Meditations*: "Meditation I"; H. H. Price, "Belief and Will," rpt. in *Belief, Knowledge and Truth*, ed. Robert R. Ammerman and Marcus G. Singer (New York: Charles Scribner's Sons, 1970), p. 59; Bertrand Russell, "Pragmatism," in *Philosophical Essays* (New York: Simon and Schuster, 1968), p. 86; A. D. Woozley, *Theory of Knowledge* (London: Hutchinson and Company, 1949), p. 185; W. K. Clifford, "The Ethics of Belief," in *Lectures and Essays*, 2 vols., ed. Leslie Stephen and Frederick Pollack (London: Macmillan, 1879).

8. This rule is limited to those beliefs for which evidence is appropriate. Thus certain beliefs about one's own state of mind, for example, might be excluded.

9. "Pragmatism," p. 86.

10. *Lectures and Essays*, 2:186.

11. See, for example, John Hick, *Philosophy of Religion* (Englewood Cliffs, N.J.: Prentice-Hall, 1963), p. 66; Bertrand Russell, *A History of Western Philosophy* (New York: Simon and Schuster, 1945), pp. 814–816.

12. See, for example, C. J. Ducasse, *A Philosophical Scrutiny of Religion* (New York: Ronald Press, 1953), pp. 160–167; Peter H. Hare and Edward H. Madden, "William James, Dickinson Miller & C. J. Ducasse on the Ethics of Belief," *Transactions of the Charles S. Peirce Society*, 4, no. 3 (Fall 1968): 115–129.

13. *WB*, p. 14.

14. *WB*, p. 20.

15. *WB*, p. 31.

16. *WB*, p. 31. See also *VRE*, p. 391.

17. I would like to thank Ms. Lynn Bortnick for this example.

18. *SR*, p. 81. See also *SR*, p. 83. James identifies this situation as one in which "faith creates its own verification." It is important, however, not to confuse this with a similar situation, which James also identifies under this same rubric—the situation in which belief in a proposition in advance of adequate evidence is necessary for arriving at the *evidence* for that proposition's truth. In this paper I call the first sort of case "faith is necessary for the fact," and the second sort of case (discussed below) "faith is necessary for the evidence."

19. *WB*, p. 29.

20. *WB*, pp. 28–29.

21. *LWL*, pp. 54–55. The truth of these examples is more easily seen when put negatively. If, for example, one believes that he will not be treated well, that he will not get the job, that he will be turned away, etc., then these beliefs will likely be self-verifying.

22. *SR*, p. 88.

23. It may, of course, be the case that in some instances of faith being necessary for the fact the believer is at the same time faced with a genuine option. In these situations the subject has two reasons, not just one, to justify his inadequately evidenced belief. Still, either reason by itself is sufficient to justify belief.

24. See *WB*, p. 15; *SR*, p. 88; *LWL*, p. 53.

25. See *WB*, p. 32n.

26. See Bertrand Russell, "Pragmatism," pp. 84–85; Wallace I. Matson, *The Existence of God* (Ithaca, N.Y.: Cornell University Press, 1965), pp. 207–208.

27. See chap. 2 above. See also *WB*, pp. 14, 32n; *LWL*, pp. 50–51.

28. *LWL*, p. 53.

29. *SR*, p. 78.

30. *SR*, p. 79n. See *WB*, pp. 25–27.

31. *WB*, pp. 31–32.

32. *WB*, p. 31. See the Christian apologist C. S. Lewis for this same point: *Mere Christianity* (New York: Macmillan, 1943), p. 58.

33. *SR*, p. 88.

34. See, for example, Thomas Kuhn, *The Structure of Scientific Revolutions*, 2d ed. (Chicago: University of Chicago Press, 1970). P. K. Feyerabend, "Explanation, Reduction, and Empiricism," in Herbert Feigl and Grover Maxwell, eds., *Minnesota Studies in the Philosophy of Science*, vol. 3 (Minneapolis: University of Minnesota Press, 1962).

35. Dickinson Miller, "'The Will to Believe' and the Duty to Doubt," *International Journal of Ethics*, 9 (1898–1899):169–195; *P*, p. 124.

36. *Philosophy of Religion*, p. 66.

37. "James's Doctrine of 'The Right to Believe,'" *The Philosophical Review*, 51, no. 6 (November 1942):552.

38. Perry, *Thought and Character*, 2:243.

39. A similar situation obtains regarding the case in which faith is necessary for the evidence. How is the subject to know, in advance of believing on faith, that faith would be justified in his situation, because it is, in fact, a case in which faith is necessary for the evidence?

6. A Pragmatic Theory of Truth

1. *P*, p. 28.

2. This is in contrast to several theories in which it is denied that the predicate "true" designates anything. See, for

example, F. P. Ramsey, "Facts and Propositions," *Proceedings of the Aristotelian Society*, supp. vol. 7 (1927):153–170; P. F. Strawson, "Truth," *Proceedings of the Aristotelian Society*, supp. vol. 24 (1950).

3. John Locke, *Essay Concerning Human Understanding*, 4, 5. Ludwig Wittgenstein, *Tractatus Logico-Philosophicus*, trans. D. F. Pears and B. F. McGuinness, (New York: Humanities Press, 1961). G. E. Moore, *Some Main Problems of Philosophy* (New York: Macmillan, 1953). Bertrand Russell, "On the Nature of Truth and Falsehood," in *Philosophical Essays*.

4. F. H. Bradley, *Essays on Truth and Reality* (Oxford: Clarendon Press, 1914); *Appearance and Reality*, 2d ed. (Oxford: Clarendon Press, 1897). B. Blanshard, *The Nature of Thought*, vol. 2 (New York: Macmillan, 1940). H. H. Joachim, *The Nature of Truth* (Oxford: Clarendon Press, 1906).

5. See for example, "A Dialogue," in *MT*, pp. 154–159. See also *MT*, pp. 68–69, 94, 128.

6. An illuminating analysis of James's views on necessary truths and the truths of the postulates of rationality has been provided by A. J. Ayer, *The Origins of Pragmatism* (San Francisco: Freeman, Cooper, 1968), pp. 195–202. See also Ellen G. Kappy, "Truth and the Justification of Belief: A Study in the Epistemology of William James" (Ph.D. dissertation, University of Wisconsin-Madison, 1972), chap. 4.

7. Perry, *Thought and Character*, 2:484–485; *MT*, p. 151.

8. *MT*, p. 96.

9. *P*, p. 97.

10. For example *P*, p. 97; *MT,* p. 109. An interesting discussion of the relationship between "verification" and "verifiability" can be found in Moreland Perkins, "Notes on the Pragmatic Theory of Truth," *Journal of Philosophy*, 49, no. 18 (August 28, 1952):573–587.

11. *MT*, p. 97; *MT*, pp. 147–148; *P*, p. 107.

12. *P*, p. 102. See *MT*, p. 91.

13. *P*, p. 99.

14. *ERE*, p. 34.

15. *MT*, p. 47. See *MT*, pp. 54–55.

16. *MT*, pp. 46–49.

17. The implications of this will be more fully considered in chap. 7.

18. *Thought and Character*, 2:476.

19. *P*, p. 96.

20. *P*, p. 102.

21. See also H. S. Thayer, *Meaning and Action*, pp. 92–93, for an illuminating discussion of James's notion of "agreement with reality."

22. *P*, p. 42.

23. See the criticisms by A. O. Lovejoy, "The Thirteen Pragmatisms," pp. 18–20; Alan R. White, *Truth* (Garden City, N.Y.: Doubleday, 1970), pp. 125–126.

24. *P*, p. 106. See also *P*, p. 44.

25. "Humanism and Truth Once More," *Mind*, n.s. 14 (1905): 190–198. See also *MT*, p. 40.

26. *MT*, pp. 113–114, 128; *P*, pp. 101, 104.

27. *P*, p. 104.

28. *P*, p. 110.

29. *P*, p. 98.

30. *MT*, p. 141; my emphasis.

31. *MT*, p. 104; see *P*, pp. 98–99; *MT*, pp. 88, 106, 112.

32. G. E. Moore, "William James' 'Pragmatism'," in *Philosophical Studies* (Paterson, N.J.: Littlefield, Adams, 1959), pp. 113–114.

33. There are several unusual instances when James goes against this stand and opts for an extreme relativism — characterizing truth in thoroughly subjective and personal terms. In these passages he maintains that the satisfactoriness of true beliefs is relative to the particular thinker's purposes and interests at a particular time, and that it makes no sense to generalize beyond these. See *PP*, 2:336n; *MT*, p. 131; *P*, p. 121. Given the extensive development of James's account of objective truth, it seems reasonable to discount these infrequent subjectivist passages.

34. *MT*, p. 89.

35. See *MT*, p. 54.

36. *MT*, pp. 54–55; *P*, p. 107.

37. *P*, pp. 106–107.

38. *P*, p. 100.

39. *P*, p. 102.

40. *MT*, pp. 143–144.

41. *ERE*, p. 13.

42. "Philosophical Conceptions," in *P*, pp. 260–261.

43. See, for example, "How to Make Our Ideas Clear," *Collected Papers,* 5.407.

44. *MT*, p. 143. See also *MT*, p. 54. Also in *P*, p. 107, where James claims that "absolute truth will have to be *made*" and appeals to the idea of eventual human agreement.

45. *P*, pp. 106–107.

46. Noteworthy is the parallelism between this conception of absolute truth as the end-point of comprehensive inter-subjective agreement and James's idea of the final ethical arrangement as the one that most inclusively satisfies all persons' demands. My objection here parallels my objection to James's ethical theory, on p. 68, that consensus is not sufficient to establish ethical value.

47. *MT*, p. 145.

48. *MT*, pp. 144–145.

49. *MT*, p. 145.

50. *P*, p. 107.

51. *P*, pp. 106–107.

52. *P*, p. 107.

53. *P*, p. 37; my emphasis.

54. *P*, p. 38.

55. *MT*, p. 48.

56. *The Origins of Pragmatism*, p. 195.

57. See *MT*, p. 141: "Empiricists think that truth in general is distilled from single men's beliefs; and the so-called pragmatists 'go them one better' by trying to define what it consists in when it comes." See also *P*, pp. 38, 116; *MT*, pp. 109–111.

58. "Introduction," in *MT*; "On William James on Truth," *Transactions of the Charles S. Peirce Society*, 13, no. 1 (Winter 1977):3–19.

59. "Introduction," in *MT*, p. xxvii.

60. See, for example, those passages, particularly when James is under critical pressure, in which he deviates from his main intent and overplays the meaning psychological and other empirical considerations have in his account. *MT*, pp. 146–147, 150.

61. *MT*, p. 89. See also pp. 94, 105, 115, 118, 120.

62. *Thought and Character*, 2:475.

63. *P*, p. 37. See *MT*, pp. 85–86, 201.

64. In *The Origins of Pragmatism* (pp. 194–195), A. J. Ayer also claims that James's interest lies in the criteria for justifying belief. From this he concludes that James was not dealing with the traditional question of (the cognitive meaning) of truth. But this fails to appreciate James's reductionism. The meaning of truth on James's view *is reducible to* the conditions of its justified ascribability.

65. Though there have been numerous objections to such a positivisitic analysis of empirical concepts. See, as examples, criticisms of Berkeley's analysis of material objects, criticisms of A. J. Ayer's early phenomenalism, or criticisms of the operationalism in the early writings of C. S. Peirce.

66. Indeed, against James's position, it has been pointed out that the concept of verifiability presupposes the concept of truth. (See for example, A. J. Ayer, *The Origins of Pragmatism*, p. 194.) To be verifiable means to be capable of being proved to be true, and thus James's analysis of truth in terms of verifiability reverses the correct relation between the two. Of course, if this is a mistake on James's theory—and I think we must say that it is—it is not merely because James ignores the relations ordinarily believed to hold between these concepts, but rather because he self-consciously offers a competing, and to his mind more plausible, analysis. The point I am making here is that James's analysis, because it fails to account for the explanatory function of the concept of truth, fails to be more plausible.

7. James's Conception of Reality

1. Chap. 21.

2. See *P*, chap. 5.

3. While in *Essays in Radical Empiricism* James's emphasis is on the metaphysical question, and while in the works mentioned above his emphasis is on pragmatic realities, both points of view can be discerned in all these works. The difference between them is a matter of emphasis and focus, not doctrine.

4. *PU*, p. xii.

5. Aside from his pragmatic writings, an important essay in which James deals with this point is "The Place of Affectional Facts in a World of Pure Experience," in *ERE*.

6. *William James* (New York: Washington Square Press, 1965), p. 144.

7. *The Origins of Pragmatism*, pp. 291–293.

8. "Pragmatism *versus* the Pragmatist," in *The Thirteen Pragmatisms and Other Essays*, p. 142. See also "Pragmatism and Realism," in *The Thirteen Pragmatisms and Other Essays*, pp. 37–39.

9. "'Pure Experience' and the External World," *Journal of Philosophy, Psychology and Scientific Methods*, 2, no. 5 (March 2, 1905):130.

10. "Natural Realism and Illusion in James's Radical Empiricism," *Transactions of the Charles S. Peirce Society*, 5 (Fall 1969):212.

11. *Introduction to William James* (Bloomington: Indiana University Press, 1967), pp. 64–65.

12. *MT*, p. 115.

13. *P*, p. 47.

14. *MT*, p. 75.

15. *MT*, pp. 42–43.

16. *MT*, p. 106.

17. Perry, *Thought and Character*, 2:536. See also *MT*, pp. 104–106; *ERE*, p. 37.

18. *MT*, p. 88.

19. For a discussion and elaboration of this idea from a phenomenological point of view, see Alfred Schuetz, "On Multiple Realities," *Philosophy and Phenomenological Research*, 5, no. 4 (June 1945):533–576.

20. *PP*, 2:291–306.

21. James clearly shows his Darwinism in the following claim that the intellectualization of experience is necessary only for the sake of fulfilling practical ends:

> The environment kills as well as sustains us. . . . Had pure experience . . . been always perfectly healthy, there would never have arisen the necessity of isolating or verbalizing any of its terms [*ERE*, p. 47].

22. *ERE*, p. 47.

23. *MT*, p. 43.

24. *P*, pp. 119–120. See also *ERE*, p. 46.

25. *MT*, p. 45. See also *P*, p. 99.

26. *MT*, p. 131. See also p. 129.

27. *P*, p. 123. See also *MT*, pp. 50–51, 57.

28. Perry, *Thought and Character*, 2:476.

29. *P*, p. 91.

30. *ERE*, p. 81.

31. *MT*, p. 7; *ERE*, p. 22.

32. For some other discussions of various aspects of James's radical empiricism, see John J. McDermott, "Introduction," in *ERE*; A. J. Ayer, *The Origins of Pragmatism*; Charlene Haddock Seigfried, *Chaos and Context: A Study in William James* (Athens: Ohio University Press, 1978).

33. *PU*, p. 113.

34. Phenomenologists have done extensive work on James's notion of the stream of experience. See, for example, Aron Gurwitsch, "William James' Theory of the 'Transitive Parts' of the Stream of Consciousness," *Philosophy and Phenomenological Research*, 3, no. 4 (June 1943):449–477. Alfred Schuetz, "William James' Concept of the Stream of Thought, Phenomenologically Interpreted," *Philosophy and Phenomenological Research*, 3 (1942–43):442–452.

35. *PU*, p. 113.

36. *ERE*, p. 69. James does not mean to suggest, however, that there is one single kind of stuff out of which pure experience is made. See *ERE*, p. 14.

37. *ERE*, p. 46.

38. He describes pure experience as "a *that* which is not yet any definite *what*, tho ready to be all sorts of whats" (*ERE*, p. 46).

39. *ERE*, p. 39. See also p. 23.

40. *ERE*, pp. 12–13.

41. *ERE*, p. 7.

42. *ERE*, pp. 6–7.

43. *ERE*, pp. 8–9.

44. See *ERE*, pp. 82–83; 92.

45. See for example, Herbert Spiegelberg, *The Phenomenological Movement* (The Hague: Martinus Nijhoff, 1965), esp. 1: 111–117. James M. Edie, "Notes on the Philosophical Anthropology of William James," in James M. Edie,

ed., *An Invitation to Phenomenology* (Chicago: Quadrangle Books, 1965). Bruce Wilshire, *William James and Phenomenology* (Bloomington: Indiana University Press, 1968). Hans Linschoten, *On the Way Toward a Phenomenological Psychology* (Pittsburgh: Duquesne University Press, 1968). James M. Edie, "William James and Phenomenology," *Review of Metaphysics*, 23, no. 3 (March 1970):481–536. D. C. Mathur, *Naturalistic Philosophies of Experience* (St. Louis: Warren H. Green, 1971). Richard Stevens, *James and Husserl: The Foundations of Meaning* (The Hague: Martinus Nijhoff, 1974). Michael Tavuzzi, "A Note on Husserl's Dependence on William James," *Journal of the British Society for Phenomenology*, 10, no. 3 (October 1979):194–196.

46. Indeed, Husserl remarks in "Persönliche Aufzeichnungen," *Philosophy and Phenomenological Research*, 16 (1956):294–295, as quoted in Spiegelberg, *The Phenomenological Movement*, 1:114:

> Then in 1891–92 came the lecture course on psychology which made me look to the literature on descriptive psychology, in fact look forward to it with longing. James's *Psychology*, of which I could read only some and very little, yielded some flashes. I saw how a daring and original man did not let himself be held down by tradition and attempted to really put down what he saw and describe it. Probably this influence was not without significance for me. . . . Indeed to describe and to be faithful, this was absolutely indispensable.

47. *ERE*, p. 46.
48. *ERE*, p. 14.
49. *ERE*, p. 13.
50. *ERE*, p. 39.
51. To see Husserl grapple with this problem, see "Fifth Meditation," *Cartesian Meditations*, trans. Dorion Cairns (The Hague: Martinus Nijhoff, 1960).
52. *ERE*, p. 39.

8. Summary and Conclusions

1. See, for example, Hilary Putnam, "Realism and Reason," *American Philosophical Association: Proceedings and Addresses*, 50, no. 6 (August 1977). Thomas S. Kuhn, *The Essen-*

tial Tension (Chicago: University of Chicago Press, 1977). Richard Rorty, *Philosophy and the Mirror of Nature* (Princeton: Princeton University Press, 1979). W. V. Quine, *Ontological Relativity and Other Essays* (New York: Columbia University Press, 1969). Nelson Goodman, *Ways of Worldmaking* (Indianapolis: Hackett Publishing Company, 1978).

Index

Absolute, the, 33–36, 45, 92, 124, 133
action, 7, 15, 20–29; and belief, 80–84; and bodily movement, 22, 27; and meaning, 37–38; and nervous-system activity, 25–27; and physiological change, 25–27; and thought, 20–29
agreement with reality, 91–92, 97, 100
Aristotle, 133
attributes, accidental, 17–20; essential, 17–20
Ayer, A. J., 117, 124–25

belief, justification of, 9–10, 69–90 passim, 146–47; on epistemic grounds, 82–86, 89–90; and irrationalism, 69–72, 85–90; on moral or prudential grounds, 74–82, 86, 89–90, 147
Bergson, Henri, 123
Berkeley, George, 53, 55–56, 124–25
Bernstein, Richard, 123

Bode, B. H., 125
British empiricists, 41

"casuistic question," in ethics, 47, 62–68
categories: of commonsense, 19, 140; for interpreting experience, 15
Clifford, W. K., 72–73
cognition, 2. *See also* reflex arc
cognitive meaning. *See* meaning
coherence theory of truth, 91–94
concepts, 133
consciousness, 134, 138, 156n
consequences of belief, and truth. *See* truth, satisfactoriness condition of

Darwinism, 2, 46, 169n
demand: as command, 50, 67–68; as felt positive interest, 49–50, 67, 159n; as judgment, 49–50, 67, 159n